LAND ROVER
Discovery

The definitive guide to **modifying**

HAYNES EXTREME

LAND ROVER
Discovery
The definitive guide to **modifying**

by **Emmeline Willmott**
and Andy Nokes

Important information

1   Advice on safety procedures and precautions is contained throughout this manual, and more specifically on page 178. You are strongly recommended to note these comments, and to pay close attention to any instructions that may be given by the parts supplier.

2   J H Haynes recommends that vehicle customisation should only be undertaken by individuals with experience of vehicle mechanics; if you are unsure as to how to go about the customisation, advice should be sought from a competent and experienced individual. Any queries regarding customisation should be addressed to the product manufacturer concerned, and not to J H Haynes, nor the vehicle manufacturer.

3   The instructions in this manual are followed at the risk of the reader who remains fully and solely responsible for the safety, roadworthiness and legality of his/her vehicle. Thus J H Haynes are giving only non-specific advice in this respect.

4   When modifying a vehicle it is important to bear in mind the legal responsibilities placed on the owners, driver and modifiers of vehicles, including, but not limited to, the Road Traffic Act 1988. IN PARTICULAR, IT IS AN OFFENCE TO DRIVE ON A PUBLIC ROAD A VEHICLE WHICH IS NOT INSURED OR WHICH DOES NOT COMPLY WITH THE CONSTRUCTION AND USE REGULATIONS, OR WHICH IS DANGEROUS AND MAY CAUSE INJURY TO ANY PERSON, OR WHICH DOES NOT HOLD A CURRENT MOT CERTIFICATE OR DISPLAY A VALID TAX DISC.

5   The safety of any alteration and its comliance with construction and use regulations should be checked before a modified vehicle is sold as it may be an offence to sell a vehicle which is not roadworthy.

6   Any advice provided is correct to the best of our knowledge at the time of publication, but the reader should pay particular attention to any changes of specification to the vehicles, or parts, which can occur without notice.

7   Alterations to vehicles should be disclosed to insurers and licensing authorities, and legal advice taken from the police, vehicle testing centres, or appropriate regulatory bodies.

8   The vehicle chosen for this project is one of those most widely customised by its owners, and readers should not assume that the vehicle manufacturers have given their approval to the modifications.

9   Neither J H Haynes nor the manufacturers give any warranty as to the safety of a vehicle after alterations, such as those contained in this book, have been made. J H Haynes will not accept liability for any economic loss, damage to property or death and personal injury arising from use of this manual other than in respect of injury or death resulting directly from J H Haynes' negligence.

© Haynes Publishing 2006

ISBN 1 84425 386 4

Printed by **J H Haynes & Co Ltd,**
Tel: 01963 442030 Fax: 01963 440001
Int. tel: +44 1963 442030 Fax: +44 1963 440001
E-mail: sales@haynes.co.uk
Web site: www.haynes.co.uk

Haynes North America, Inc
861 Lawrence Drive, Newbury Park, California 91320, USA

Editions Haynes
4, Rue de l'Abreuvoir
92415 COURBEVOIE CEDEX, France

Haynes Publishing Nordiska AB
Box 1504, 751 45 UPPSALA, Sweden

(4386 - 184)

Contents

Introduction 4
A star was born . . . 5
Model history 6
Off-road expeditions – planning your trip 8
Driving off-road – tips and techniques 12
Getting unstuck 13
Waffle boards 14
Ground anchors 14
Land Rover experience centres 15

Engine
Electric fan 18
Snorkel raised air intake 25
Silicone hoses and Hiclones 30
Intercooler and silicone turbo pipes 32
Exhaust 35

Underside
Rock sliders/jackable sills 40
Dan bar 43
Sump/steering guard 44
Diff guards 46
Fuel tank guard 49
Air locker differential 52
Air compressor 62
Air line for tyre inflation 67
Land Meter aka clinometer or pitch 'n' roll meter 68

Suspension
Multi-shocks 72
Front suspension 74
Extended brake lines 76
Rear suspension 84
Rear dislocation cones 89
Bush renewal 90
Air cylinder installation 91

Bodywork
Removing wheels 'n' jacking up 96
Wheels and tyres 98
Spare wheel carrier 98
Rear bumper 100
Rear cradle and winch 104
Front bumper 108
Front winch 110
Weathershields 114
Roll cages 115
Nudge/roo bar 116
Rear step 117
Roof rack 118
Wheel arch extension kit 119
Custom panels 122
Chequer plate 123
Customising bonnet 126
Customising load areas 128
Bush wires 132
Rear ladder 134
Tinting windows 136

Electrical system
Split charge system 142
230V inverter with 3-pin socket 146
12V sockets in load area 148
Auxiliary fusebox 149
Nudge bar mounted lights 152
Bonnet pod lights 153
Headlamp protection grilles 158
Rear light cluster protection grilles 160
Roof-mounted front lights 162
Roof-mounted rear working light 166
CB radio and antenna 168
Distance/trip meter 174
Satellite navigation 177

Reference
Safety 178
Modifications and the Law 180

Introduction

Before …

The market in Land Rover modifying parts is massive, with a vast array of components available for today's vehicles. The aim is the same, to improve on the standard vehicle and give it an individual identity – the difference is in the financial investment.

The aim of this book is to show how to fit many of the popular aftermarket components, and in the Haynes tradition, to pass on the hints and tips gained from doing the work ourselves. Fitting instructions are supplied with most aftermarket parts; a few are comprehensive and supported by further information on their maker's websites, but others either assume a high level of knowledge on the part of the owner.

The fitting of most aftermarket components will require a certain amount of dismantling, and the procedures for doing so are not always immediately obvious. A workshop manual will provide torque setting data and in the case of fitting electrical components access to a full wiring diagram will prove invaluable.

When choosing parts, take time to read product reviews in the press and consult the leading suppliers; most have websites and catalogues and are happy to discuss fitments. It's a good idea to retain all the original equipment parts you replace because future owners may prefer to revert some components back to standard form.

Having modified your Discovery you are required to declare your modifications when seeking insurance cover. This applies particularly if the modification increases the power of the vehicle and alters its performance. If you have had a one-off paint job done, you may find that the insurance company will not insure due to the high cost of replicating a damaged panel. Some mainstream insurance providers may not look upon modifications too kindly, though there are a number of insurers that do understand people with Land Rovers and the desire to modify them, and will provide insurance for your vehicle with all modifications listed for not a great deal more than you would pay for a standard vehicle. It remains to be said that you must be honest about your work, but in your favour discounts are available for any security devices that are fitted, limited mileage policies and being a member of an owners' club, so make sure you mention these when seeking a quote. These types of insurers regularly advertise in many Land Rover magazines.

… and after

Land Rover's aim to bridge the gap between the utilitarian Defender 90/110 and the luxurious, expensive, Range Rover, whilst introducing a British rival to the established Japanese models, was finally fulfilled by the conception of the Discovery, codenamed 'Project Jay', in 1986. Launched at the Frankfurt motor show in November 1989, the Discovery became almost overnight one of the nation's most loved mid-range, off-road vehicles, targeting the passenger comfort and family 4X4 market, a *market that at this time barely existed!* Off-road testers were quick to accredit the Discovery as best vehicle in its class and the motoring press raved about the new model. The public, impressed by what it had heard, soon started to pile into showrooms. A waiting list had been necessary from day one, but even so the Discovery took little time in becoming the best selling 4X4 leisure vehicle in the UK. A clear indication that, once again, Land Rover had designed and built a vehicle that people wanted.

Capable of competing against a family car in terms of comfort, the Discovery certainly did not lack the power and performance the model range required, using the now-famous Rover 3.5i V8 engine in carburettor form. The diesel option was a brand new 2.5i direct-injection intercooled turbo-diesel unit engineered specifically for the vehicle, known as the 200Tdi. Whilst this unit boasted impressive economy and best in class performance, it was noted as being slightly noisier than rival manufacturers' diesels. Later on this unit was used in the Range Rover Classic and the Defender.

The Discovery was in many ways more of an evolutionary development born of the Range Rover Classic than a truly new vehicle, sharing a close mechanical relationship with this earlier breed. Sitting on a 100 inch wheelbase taken directly from the Range Rover it also utilised the same long-travel coil suspension, axles, permanent 4WD transmission, high/low transfer box, excellent ground clearance and V8 engine – the Boge self-levelling suspension was not fitted to the Discovery due to the design complexity and cost.

An interesting fact to note is that, whilst based on the Range Rover chassis, the Series 1 Discovery is actually longer, taller and heavier. The increased height at the rear of the Discovery was to provide more headroom necessary for passengers sitting on the pull-down side seats in the 'boot'. The stepped roofline, rather than just a direct copy of the

Daihatsu Fourtrak that was released before the Disco, was made individual by incorporating a roof light either side. These innovative windows had the effect of creating a lighter and more spacious cabin, and rear passengers benefited from a more panoramic view of the countryside rather than vision limited to two headrests! Because the Discovery was higher than the Range Rover, designers decided to try an optical illusion – cutting off the rear of the vehicle sharply (compared with the Range Rover's angled back), this not only disguised the height but made the vehicle look shorter too. The extra height meant that the Disco would have a steel roof rather than aluminium, to give extra structural strength to the taller car. Parts from other models such as Sherpa van headlights, BL switchgear, Maestro van tail lamps and Morris Marina door handles all helped to cut project costs considerably.

One of the most unusual features about the earliest Discoverys is the fact that they were only available in a 3-door format. At the time it seemed there were concerns about the rigidity of a 5-door body when driving off-road. This would provide a perfect explanation of why the Discovery, a model engineered specifically for the family market, was initially only available with three doors. Aside from the criticism over door count, the Discovery was a distinctive-looking model with attractive styling and visually unlike rival 4X4s in any way, except for the overall size of the vehicle. This model range, unlike the original Land Rovers, was aimed at those people who wanted a 4X4 for everyday transport (either for usefulness or for the trendy image that had developed through the eighties), with no loss in comfort or equipment levels. And it was certainly well-equipped with added luxuries such as electric windows, central locking, electrically-adjustable door mirrors, alloy wheels and seating for up to seven people. At approximately £17,000 it was competitively priced against some top-of-the-range Japanese models.

Nine months after the launch of the range, the extremely popular 5-door model was introduced, bringing with it a whole host of other improvements to the Discovery in general, such as fuel injection on the V8 engine, offering improved performance and increased top speed. These changes transformed an already excellent machine into an even better one.

In the early days hard-core Land Rover enthusiasts dismissed the Discovery because of its body styling, even though the vehicle was every bit as tough as anything else that rolled off the production lines at the factory in Solihull. Today many of those early critics are themselves using and enjoying the Discovery for everyday and quite serious off-road use. Its styling, along with efficient Tdi power plants, ensured that the Discovery became the most successful vehicle of its time, regularly spotted on British roads. Popular as the original Range Rover was, it never measured up to the success of the Discovery – our nation's favourite.

Discovery 1 – 1989 to 1998

At the launch, the Discovery was only available as a 3-door version, although a 5-door version followed shortly. The stepped roofline was quite a distinctive styling cue and this particular feature has been carried through to the very latest models. The target to bridge the gap between the Range Rover and Defender had been met well. Engines available were the 3.5 litre V8, the 2.5 litre 200Tdi and a 2 litre MPI engine, though on balance this latter engine was never really suitable for a Discovery as the fuel economy was akin to the V8 and the performance was poor on and off road. The Tdi and V8 gave acceptable performance and both suited heavy-duty towing.

Using running gear and wheelbase similar to that of the Range Rover, the Discovery was a dream to drive on and off-road. Its long coil springs kept all four wheels in ground contact, much better than that of rival manufacturers' vehicles.

In 1994 a facelift was carried out to keep the model range fresh. The V8 engine capacity was increased to 3.9 litres and a revised diesel power unit was installed, called the 300Tdi. Many of the improvements were to reduce the noise, vibration and harshness found in the 200 series engine. A revised gearbox was introduced with significant improvements in gearshift quality. Cosmetic changes included new headlamps, indicators, grille, and revised bumper mouldings.

The rear bumper was noticeably changed with the addition of lights being fitted into it. Inside the cabin, a new dashboard was introduced, with separate temperature controls for both driver and passenger. On some models air bags were introduced. New fabrics gave a fresh look, whilst levels of passenger comfort were increased with heated seats, cruise control and heated front screen (top spec models). People wanting ultimate luxury without paying Range Rover prices quickly snapped up the higher spec models.

Discovery 2 – 1998 to 2004

The series 2 Discovery was introduced in 1998 with major changes over and above the earlier models. Engines available

were the V8, this time in 4.0 litre form, and the all new TD5 power plant. The TD5 was much smoother than the outgoing 300Tdi engine, and produced a significant increase in power output. Underneath the vehicle, Land Rover reduced the amount of body roll when cornering by fitting rear air suspension and active corner enhancement (ACE) – fitted to top spec models. This hydraulic system takes a reading from sensors around the vehicle and responds to roll by increasing the pressure in the rams on the side of the vehicle that is likely to lean; doing all of this before any roll actually takes place. Handling and stability was improved by fitting wider axles to increase the vehicle's track width and by the addition of electronic traction control (ETC). This did away with the familiar diff lock, although the mechanisms were still present in the transfer box, it just wasn't connected anymore. However, due to high public demand, it was re-introduced on the 2003 models.

Inside, the cabin was as spacious as ever – the dash layout remained very similar to the 300 series, but the third row of seats idea was given a re-think. Although they were still of the 'fold away when not in use' type, instead of having to sit sideways, passengers could now benefit from facing in a forward direction. The other seats were also redesigned to give better support and with adjustable head restraints.

Discovery 3 – 2004 to present day

The all new Discovery, introduced in 2004, bore little similarity to the previous model range. The stepped roof line, though now reduced, is one of the only styling cues that remained. The engines changed once more – still a V8 option but capacity increased to 4.4 litres. Another all-new diesel power plant, this time a V6 diesel or TDV6 as it's known, 2.7 litres in capacity. Both engines have enough torque to tow any trailer even though the vehicle's kerb weight is over 2.5 tonnes.

Driving a 200 series Discovery required a lot of driver input, especially if enthusiastic driving was required, but the new Discovery can be hurtled around twisting country lanes with relative ease. Cross-linked independent air suspension will account for most of this, though base models will still have the coil spring suspension.

Inside the cabin has dramatically changed also. Still a seven-seater, but the rearmost seats, when not in use, fold away into the floor giving a flat load area. There are electronics aplenty at the front of the vehicle, the centre console housing a satellite navigation system, which shows where you are positioned off-road, as well as showing contour lines. There is also a display that will show you what each wheel is doing when off-road, ie, whether the diffs are locked, angle of steering, etc. Another new feature, called the Terrain Response System, is operated using a dial on the centre console. Five different settings allow you to dial in the type of

terrain you are driving over, and then the engine, transmission and suspension settings are all re-configured to suit maximum performance for that terrain.

In short, this is the most technologically advanced Discovery yet and certainly a long way from the early 200 series Discovery, yet brought together in the fact that they are all great performers on and off road.

Destination

Planning and preparing your vehicle is just one part of the organisational process you go through when planning any kind of off-road trip. Other concerns such as protecting your health, right up to ensuring you have the correct documentation, can apply to even the most basic off-road trips.

Once you have decided on your destination you must learn as much as possible about the area – the local customs, any rules and regulations you may encounter, what you will require, which health precautions are necessary, the route you should take, and the terrain you will encounter when travelling. Nowhere in the world is out of bounds for an off-road trip, though needless to say the better-equipped and well-trained driver can go farther afield. If you are contemplating shipping your vehicle to a foreign country and then going on an overland expedition, consider the climate changes that happen there in a typical year. Research your route from at least three separate sources so that you are aware of areas of poor infrastructure. The last thing you need is to get caught in an area in the rainy season where any chance of forward progress is severely hampered by the weather, and where the nearest dock to pick up a container ship takes days of travelling to get to.

Personal health

When on expedition, remember to take care of yourself as well as your kit. Before leaving for a long-term expedition, make sure you have a full medical and dental check. Eat and drink safely – wherever you travel always ensure you have enough clean water; in hot arid conditions you should allow six to eight litres daily intake of water per person, four litres per person in more wintry conditions. Medical insurance is essential.

Take care in the sun, avoid insect and animal bites and take precautions against major diseases such as malaria – you should consult your doctor at least two months before you depart for advice on immunisations, as some cannot be given in conjunction with others, whilst some take several stages of injections to be administered properly, and some just take time to become effective. Note that the cost of such immunisations can be quite high, especially if there are a number of your family travelling with you. There are many websites that can help you with personal advice on travelling abroad, for example www.doh.gov.uk/traveladvice. These websites will help you understand what, if any, immunisations are required and how to get treatment abroad if necessary.

Carry a first aid kit at all times – a basic kit must include adhesive dressings, insect repellent, antiseptic cream, and water purification tablets. An emergency medical travel kit containing sterilised, sealed items such as syringes, needles, suture materials, intravenous set and blood substitute solution, may also be a good idea. There are specialist travel clinics that sell personalised first aid kits to save you the effort of procuring some of these items. Remember to ensure that the drugs you carry do not have restrictions in the countries you are visiting – the Home Office Drugs branch will be able to help you further with this. If you take prescription medicines, do not remove them from the original packaging, and make sure you have enough.

Before preparing and eating food, especially in the more far-flung places, wash your hands thoroughly using three bowls: the first with soap and water, the second with disinfectant solution and finally rinse with plain water. It might seem over the top, but it's a lot better than a gastric upset.

Always be prepared for adverse weather conditions. Wear several thin layers of comfortable fabric that dries easily so these can be removed one by one as the temperature rises or if you get wet. A waterproof coat should be packed. Ensure you take suitable precautions against extreme weather conditions by wearing such things as high factor sun cream and a hat. Quality, lightweight, comfortable boots are a necessity.

Money

Expedition costs will vary according to the location and your lifestyle on the road. If you camp using a tent and prepare your own meals it should be easier to keep costs down. When on expedition or exploration you should earmark some money for vehicle repair bills en route. The amount will largely depend on the age and condition of your vehicle, your location and route. It's best to speak with a Land Rover specialist who will advise you on parts that are prone to wear and the spare items you should be carrying as part of your basic kit. If you are partaking in extreme off-roading, your vehicle's body protection should already be extensive.

When travelling deep in the bush be aware that it may be difficult to cash travellers cheques, and credit card facilities

may be restricted to tourist areas, so carry enough cash as is safely possible in a mixture of small and large notes. US dollars are widely accepted everywhere in the world so take these as a safeguard if you are travelling across lots of countries and run out of one particular currency. Remember to split the money up and hide it in a variety of lockable locations within the vehicle.

Kit

Storage boxes in different sizes, clearly marked with their contents are useful. Food, perishables, first aid equipment and documentation should always be carried in water and dust-proof containers. Make sure that kit does not rub or rattle together. You can purchase a lot of kit from army surplus stores, including weight and space-saving items, such as thin metal pans that stack inside each other. If your budget will allow it, a fridge freezer is an excellent item of equipment to buy, just make sure the vehicle's electrics will cope with powering it.

Water can be carried in plastic containers that won't affect the water quality in any way. Stainless steel water tanks may carry the water easily, but once contaminated are very difficult to clean out. If your water source is from a lake or river it makes filling the tank awkward. Water must always be purified before drinking and using for cooking.

Camping kit must be of good quality. Most off-roaders use a fold-up tent that mounts on the roof rack – the mattress stows away inside it. They can be erected and dismantled quickly and most have built-in mosquito nets. In areas that are prone to heavy rainfall, and snakes and other dangerous creatures, camping on the roof of your vehicle is preferable, and the tents are designed to perform well in all weather conditions. Take bedding that suits you and the climate you are travelling in, as sometimes standard EU camping gear is not quite good enough.

Awnings can be fixed to roof racks to provide shade and additional sleeping quarters if needed.

A basic kit list for expedition use should include the following items:
- Good compass, GPS if possible.
- Maps and guide books of the area.
- Plastic bags for storage and waste.
- Three bowls for washing hands, hand soap and a suitable disinfectant.
- Washing up bowl and washing up liquid.
- Toilet paper, cleaning cloths and tea towels.
- Spare prescription glasses and sunglasses.
- Fresh water tanks.
- Fire extinguisher.
- Matches/disposable lighters.
- Powdered milk.
- Can opener.

- Kettle with lid, pans, frying pan.
- Tinned food with minimal water content.
- Plastic plates, bowls, cups, stainless steel cutlery.
- Knives and cooking utensils.
- Folding chairs and table.
- Mosquito and other insect repellents.
- Sleeping bag.
- Washing line (or use bush wires, if fitted) and pegs.
- Mosquito net.
- Torch and spare batteries.
- Scissors, pen and paper.
- Tool kit.
- Spares and repairs kit.
- Shovel and saw.
- Puncture repair kit.
- Recovery kit.
- Medical and first aid kit.
- Clothing to suit the climate you are travelling in.
- Toiletries and towel.
- Water purification tablets.
- Universal adhesive or silicone sealant.

Preparation of your vehicle

No matter how good the standard vehicle is, you must still prepare it properly for any off-road and expedition use – every process shown in this book is an important part of achieving this. It is an added bonus if one member of the party has mechanical knowledge and has the relevant Haynes workshop manual to hand to assist with any repairs that may be required both before you set off and off-road.

Make sure the vehicle has had a recent full service, where

brakes, clutch, suspension and steering are scrutinised and that the timing belt/chain (when applicable) has been replaced. Make sure there are no oil leaks and that all bushes, bearings and joints are sound. Get to know the vehicle so that you can recognise when something has failed or needs attention. Any additional equipment should have been fitted in advance to enable you to become familiar with it in the event of any problems arising. This equipment should be securely fastened so that, even with constant vibration from uneven road surfaces, it does not work free. Regularly check and retighten retaining bolts, screws and nuts. Some parts such as the suspension may need to be upgraded to cope with the extra load the vehicle will carry and driving over aggressive, uneven terrain.

Dust will certainly get everywhere no matter what country you travel in. A raised air intake is a necessity to pull cleaner air into the engine. A raised intake will also help to prevent water ingress when crossing deep-water sections.

Don't run out of fuel – always carry jerry cans that will see you through more remote areas where filling stations will be sparse. Additional fuel tanks can be fitted at a higher cost. Remember in third world countries it will be necessary to filter the fuel as it goes into the tank, especially if it is from cans – specialised filter funnels or additional in-line fuel filters can also be fitted to help with this task. Ensure that all additional fuel is carried safely. It is recommended that you carry more

fuel than you anticipate using so that you can cope with any problems that may arise such as getting lost.

The vehicle's electrical system must be well-installed and a split charge dual or triple battery system must be fitted if you are to even contemplate any off-road expedition.

Tyres, including spares, must be in perfect condition. Most off-roaders will run an additional airline to the rear of the car from a compressor, to inflate the tyres if the pressures have been lowered for driving over soft terrain.

You must ensure you have at least one secure place in which you store valuables such as passports, other documentation and currency. Custom built secure drawers in the load area that are disguised is one good way of doing this. It must not be obvious to thieves where your valuables are stored.

Once off-road, regular maintenance checks must be carried out. These include: oil and fluid levels and leaks, tightness of fixings on all bolted down equipment, air filter, grease prop shafts, tyres, brakes, lights and all other electrics.

Paperwork and regulations

The following list of will give you an insight into the extent of paperwork you must carry, particularly if you are visiting countries outside the UK. Give yourself plenty of time to gather the relevant documentation before leaving home – don't leave it until the last minute!

If you are visiting a country that requires a visa it is preferable to get that sorted before you leave home. Sometimes visas have a very short shelf life. Some countries have other entry requirements you must meet; for more information refer to *Driving abroad* from Haynes Publishing.

A passport must be carried at all times and be valid until at least 6 months after your return home. Take photocopies of your passport and leave one copy at home with someone you can contact in case of an emergency. Your passport must have enough pages free – you should allow one page per country for stamps and visas.

One of the most expensive and important documents you will require is a Carnet de Passage – required to temporarily import a vehicle duty-free into certain countries outside the EU which normally require a deposit against import charges. The document is only available from the RAC and its application must be supported by a bank guarantee, cash deposit and insurance policy. 50% of the premium is refundable when the Carnet is returned to the RAC at the end of your expedition. The booklet is available in 5, 10 or 25 page format, the 5 page booklet allowing you to import a vehicle into 5 countries or on 5 different occasions, and so on. It is vital that the pages of the Carnet are correctly endorsed at the borders of the country you are entering and exiting, as they prove that the

vehicle has complied with temporary import requirements and remove the possibility for any future import charges. The cash deposit will depend on the rates of the customs duty and taxes in the countries you are visiting and the value of your vehicle. Once the RAC has received a completed application form with these details, they will provide a no-obligation quotation.

An International Certificate of Motor Vehicles (ICMV) is essentially a passport for your vehicle (an internationally recognised registration document), available from the RAC for around £4.00. It is not usually compulsory, but can ease you through borders, as the more documents you have the more impressed customs will be. Note that you should also take your V5 document as well as an ICMV.

The International Driving Permit (IDP), commonly referred to as the international driving licence, is proof that you hold a valid driving licence in your own country. It may not always be a necessity to carry one, although, as it is printed in ten languages and provides photographic identification, it can be advantageous. The IDP costs around £4.00 and is available from the AA and RAC. Their websites have forms that can be downloaded so that you can apply for a 12 month permit. You may apply for an IDP a maximum of 3 months before your departure date, but not when already abroad. Be sure to carry your UK driving licence when on expedition as well as the IDP.

Valid road tax and an MOT certificate should be carried with you at all times. Unless the vehicle has been permanently exported, it is required to comply with British legislation when abroad. Both of these documents must still be in date once you return home.

A GB sticker must be displayed at all times on any UK registered motor vehicle driven abroad.

The Green Card, available from your UK car insurance company, will provide proof of insurance cover when driving through Europe. All UK car insurance policies provide the minimum level of cover legally required in EU countries, and the Green Card illustrates that you have met the local requirements. You will need to extend your policy to travel outside of the EU; you may have to buy local cover as you go. Few insurance companies offer policies that will cover your own vehicle for theft and/or damage outside Europe. For third party liability, local insurance can be purchased either at the borders or main towns of the country you are visiting. If you are able to find a company that will provide third party cover for all of Europe and Africa it is a good idea to arrange the policy before you leave home. It may prove a more costly way of securing insurance, but you will not have the inconvenience of trying to buy it at the borders or waiting and driving uninsured until you reach a big town.

Medical insurance is essential. Consider what level of cover you may require – the general rule is more cover the better. There are companies that specifically cater for the needs of travellers so you can shop around to find the best deals.

Driving off-road – tips and techniques

The Discovery is a sure favourite in Camel trophy events and other demanding off-road trials due to its incredible off-road credentials. However, if extreme off-road events are out of your league and your preference lies with the less aggressive green lane trips instead, remember to follow this polite code of conduct established by the Green Lane Association (GLASS) for guidance when driving in the countryside.

Use only rights of way with known, proven or provable vehicle rights. If challenged, discuss and if not resolved, leave as requested until further investigation is made.

Keep to the defined track. Detour only to pass immovable obstructions. Report any obstructions to the local highway authority. It is your right to remove non-lawful obstructions, but make sure you have the ability and equipment to do so before attempting it.

If the route is not obvious on the ground, ask locally, check maps held at the local highway authority offices or consult the local GLASS area representative.

Travel at a quiet and unobtrusive pace and as slowly as is practical. Ensure your vehicle is fully road legal; un-surfaced rights of ways (URoWs) are subject to the same laws as surfaced roads.

When travelling in groups keep to a small number. Split large parties up and use a different route or allow a good interval to elapse before following.

Do not travel on un-surfaced roads when they risk being affected beyond a natural point of recovery once the weather improves. If need be, walk the route first to determine its suitability. Take into account the tyres that you or others are using, and the equipment you carry.

Avoid damage to trees, hedgerows and boundaries. Some

roads carry vehicular rights but are physically too narrow for 4X4s.

Be courteous to other road users – pull over and stop for walkers. Pull over and stop your engine for passing horses. Thank those that have moved over for you.

Use recovery techniques such as a winch with extreme caution and only use the correct equipment.

If gates are found open they should be left open. Those that are found shut or swinging should be shut behind you. The land owner may appreciate being told about a gate that is insecure.

Keep dogs and children under supervision. Watch out for injured or trapped animals and report all suspicious events to the land owner.

Guard against all risks of fire.

Take your litter home and that left by others wherever possible. Plastic bags can suffocate livestock if swallowed.

Remember that wild life already faces many threats and URoWs are valuable habitats, so take special care in spring and early summer.

When driving off-road keep your seatbelts tight – drivers are often surprised how much they get bounced around, the seatbelt may prevent some bumps and bruising.

Stay relaxed whilst driving – sit up straight but leave your arms, legs and neck relaxed to absorb vibrations that will come through the suspension.

Keep a light grip on the steering wheel as it can kick back suddenly when you hit a rock, hole or other obstacle. A light grip will prevent your hands from getting hurt. Also, keep your thumbs and fingers on the outside diameter of the steering wheel, since the spokes can really hurt you on a kickback.

Conserve your brakes on long hill descents, select a low gear and use engine braking to keep your speed down – use the 'Low' range of your transfer case.

Nothing can ruin a great day off-road as fast as getting stuck in the mud or sand. Worse still is getting stuck in the middle of a big hill! The best advice we can give is to not get stuck in the first place, but it's bound to happen sooner or later. To minimise the risk of getting stuck, don't slow down or stop when you're on soft surfaces. If you're not sure you can make it up a hill, don't try.

When you first realise you're stuck, it's best just to get out of the vehicle and take a few minutes to relax and let your anger subside. Don't just sit there and rev the engine – you could get yourself stuck worse or damage the vehicle. Look under the vehicle at the front, rear and on both sides. Most of the time, you'll find that one or more of your wheels have sunk into the soft stuff. But sometimes you'll also find the chassis hung up on a tree stump, rock or other obstruction. It's important to know exactly what the problem is. If you're stuck on an obstruction, you'll have to get the vehicle up above the obstruction before you drive out. If you don't, you're likely to rip a hole through your sump or fuel tank.

If it's just your wheels that are stuck, and if you're not too deep into the stuff, try 'bouncing' the vehicle at the end that's stuck. This approach requires one or two helpers – the bigger the better! While you're in the vehicle, use the throttle gently, have your helpers bounce the suspension up and down by pushing on the bumper. The increase in downward pressure can often be just enough for you to regain traction and get unstuck. But be careful – if your helpers are bouncing on the back bumper, only use forward gears. If they're at the front, only use reverse. Don't take a chance – your vehicle may suddenly get traction and run over your friends.

If you can drive a short distance before finally losing traction, you might also try 'rocking' the vehicle back and forth. Drive it forward as far as it will go, apply the brakes, drive it in reverse as far as it will go, apply the brakes, then repeat. This way you might build up enough inertia to finally roll out of the rut.

Still stuck? Try some traction aids. If you're in snow or ice, sand or gravel works very well – just spread it in front of the stuck wheel(s). If you're in mud, use rocks, pieces of tree branches or other non-slippery items. If you're in sand, try to spread the load over a wide area: a large piece of wood or a few large rocks will often do the trick. And with any traction aid, it's going to work best if you level-out the area in front of the wheel first (you did bring your shovel, right?).

If you're stuck in some really big ruts, or if the vehicle is stuck on an obstruction, try jacking it up until the wheel is out of its rut. You can then fill in the rut with gravel, tree branches or similar material. If the chassis is stuck on an obstruction, jack the wheel up as far as possible and put rocks under the tyre to effectively raise the vehicle above the obstruction.

If there's another vehicle in the area that's not stuck,

you're really in luck. Just take out your tow-rope (don't leave the road without one). Hook it between solid, rounded points, such as recovery points or a trailer-hitch. Don't hook the rope around a bumper or other sharp-edged object that could cut the rope. Stay out of the way while using a tow rope, since it could break suddenly.

When all else fails, it's time to hook up your winch to the nearest solid anchor (if it's a live tree, use a trunk guard to protect it) and pull yourself out. Don't have a power winch? Well, you should at least carry a hand winch that's rated to handle the weight of your vehicle. Pulling your vehicle out with a one of these is a slow, sweaty process, but it usually beats walking.

Waffle boards

These are a relatively new type of design of traction aid based on the floor grids of an oil rig, and are one of the most useful off-road pieces of kit you can buy. They are made from interwoven glass reinforced plastic so are non-porous and will not rust. They are totally flexible and after use will return to their original shape.

Weighing in at approximately 7 kgs each, they are lightweight and easy to handle, despite this they can support a fully-laden Discovery. They are strong enough to use as bridging ladders to cross ditches and gulleys, or can be used in deep ruts or sand to prevent your vehicle from becoming stuck. A neat, simple traction solution that is essential to your off-road kit.

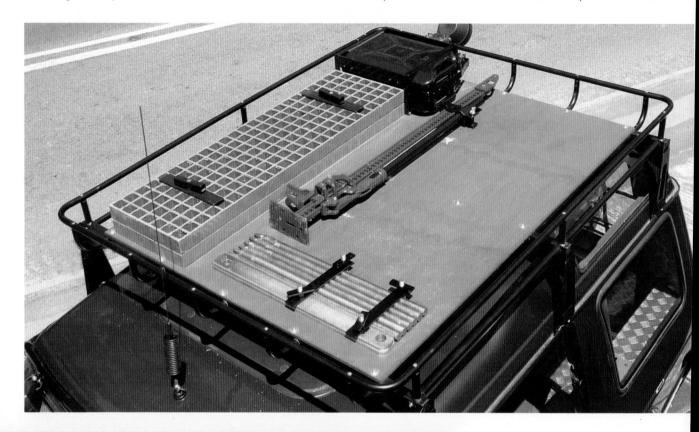

Ground anchors

These are for use when other suitable anchor points are not available for recovery, such as trees or large rocks. They are available in several forms:

Augers
- These are usually about 4 ft in length and are screwed into the ground if it is soft.

Pickets
- Made from wood or angled iron and driven into the ground. Several of

these can be used in a line and tied together. Tie the head of the front picket to the base of the next.

Spare wheel
- Your spare wheel can be used for this purpose if buried in the ground at the right angle to the line of pull.

Danforth anchors
- Small boat type anchors of Danforth design. These work as the

self-burying type but require somebody to stand on them as they first 'bite'.

Pull–Pal
- Similar in design to the Danforth anchor, but is an American folding design by Pat Gromillion. As above they require somebody to stand on them as they first 'bite' until firm. When finished with, they are quite easy to remove if they are pushed onto their side and pulled out.

To learn more about driving off-road safely, the patrons of off-roading, Land Rover, have established a number of experience centres (listed below) around the UK. At these centres you can take part in courses on winching and trailer handling, GPS navigation, as well as extensive 4X4 training, and fun off-road driving days, in all modern Land Rover vehicles including the Discovery.

Land Rover Experience West Country
Wessington Farm
Awliscombe, Nr Honiton
Devon EX14 3NU
Tel: 0870 26 444 71
E-mail: info@lre9.co.uk

Land Rover Experience Chilterns
Hounslow Hall Estate
Newton Longville
Milton Keynes MK17 0BU
Tel: 0870 26 444 65
Fax: 0870 26 444 66
E-mail: info@lre6.co.uk

Land Rover Experience South East
Eastwell Court, Eastwell Park
Lenacre Street
Ashford
Kent TN25 4JT
Tel: 0870 26 444 67
Fax: 0870 26 444 68
E-mail: info@lre7.co.uk

Land Rover Experience Malverns
Eastnor Castle
Ledbury, Herefordshire
Tel: 0870 26 444 69
Fax: 0870 26 444 70
E-mail: info@lre8.co.uk

Land Rover Experience East Of England
Rockingham Castle
Market Harborough
Leicestershire
LE16 8TH
Tel: 0870 26 444 63
Fax: 0870 26 444 64
E-mail: info@lre5.co.uk

Land Rover Experience North Yorkshire
The Cabin
Coniston Hall Estate
Nr Skipton
North Yorkshire
Tel: 0870 26 444 59
E-mail: info@lre3.co.uk

Land Rover Experience Snowdonia
Pale Hall, Pale Estate
Llandderfel, Nr Bala
Gwynedd LL23 7PS
Tel: 0870 26 444 61
Fax: 0870 26 444 62
E-mail info@lre4.co.uk

Land Rover Experience Scotland
Dunkeld Resort Hotel
Dunkeld
Perthshire
Tel: 0870 26 444 55
Fax: 0870 26 444 56
E-mail: info@lre1.co.uk

Land Rover Experience Northern Ireland
Clandeboye Courtyard
Bangor
Co. Down
Tel: 0870 26 444 57
Fax: 0870 26 444 58
E-mail: info@lre2.co.uk

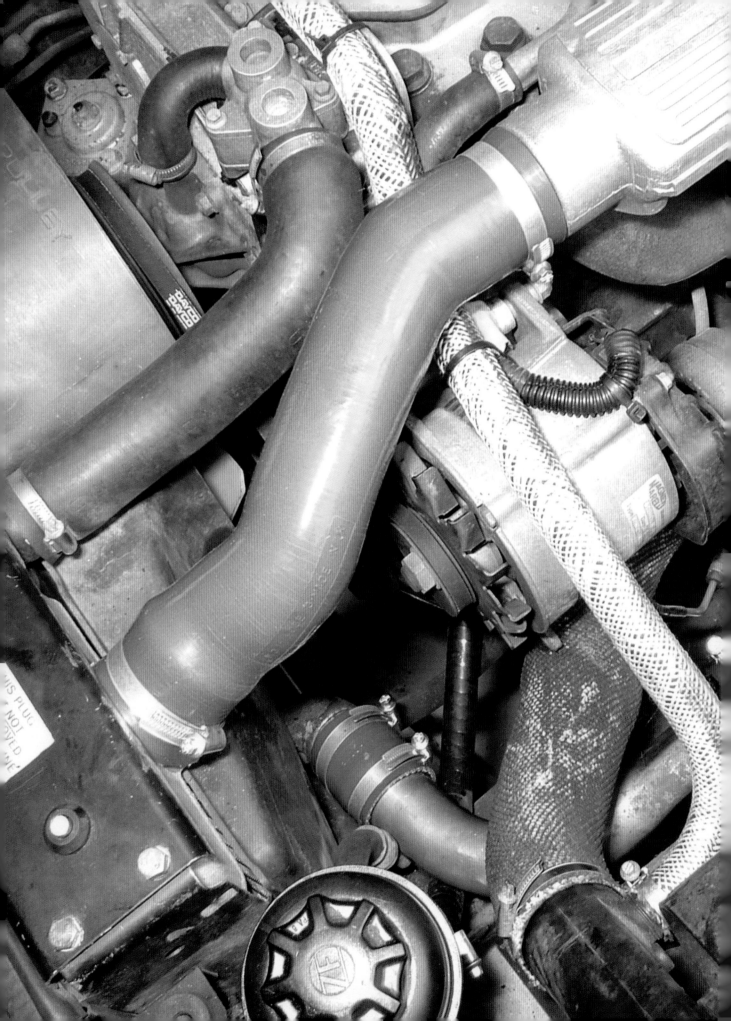

ENGINE

Electric fan

Snorkel raised air intake

Silicone hoses and Hiclones

Intercooler and
silicone turbo pipes

Exhaust

Electric fan

A standard Discovery is fitted with a viscous coupled fan, which most of the time is not required until the engine gets hot enough for the coupling to 'lock up' and additional air is drawn through the radiator to aid cooling. The only times that a viscous fan is likely to be neded is when sitting in stationary traffic, or moving very slowly when the engine is under increased load such as towing a heavy trailer. The rest of the time the fan is largely redundant. The energy the engine uses to turn this fan when it is not needed is wasteful of fuel, and switching to an electric version is a good idea because it will save fuel, decrease engine noise (when not in operation) and reduce engine warm-up time.

In this procedure we are fitting a Kenlow fan as a replacement to the existing viscous fan, and not as an additional one. We removed the radiator from the vehicle for simplicity, but this is not necessary. The fan is controlled by a capillary unit inserted into the top radiator hose to measure coolant temperature. A variable dial is supplied to set the temperature at which the fan is required to 'cut-in'.

It should be noted that in an off-road type of application it is necessary to add an isolation switch in the feed for the fan motor (see wiring diagram). The reason for this is to switch off the supply to the motor for crossing deep water sections. If the fan were to 'cut-in' whilst in water the motor would not be strong enough to move the water and would blow the fuse in the supply or cause damage to the motor itself. In our installation we made the illumination inside the isolation switch come on when the supply was cut off to warn the driver that the fan was out of operation and to turn it back on as soon as the water section had been crossed. Failure to turn the supply back on may lead to overheating later, so it is important to have a warning device incorporated into this installation.

1 Undo the radiator filler plug, then syphon as much of the coolant out of the radiator as is possible. We shall be removing the radiator from the vehicle in order to fit the replacement fan, and all of the coolant will be drained, so make sure you have something in place under the vehicle to catch the coolant as the hoses are removed. Make sure the coolant is cold before doing this to reduce the danger of scalding.

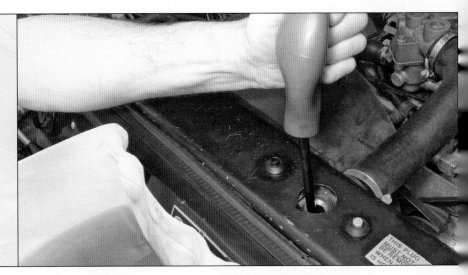

2 Remove the top radiator hose.

3 Using a fan hub spanner, remove the viscous coupling retaining nut. It has a **left-hand thread**.

4 Remove the fan assembly from the vehicle

5 Unscrew the two nuts and washers or clips that secure the upper cooling fan cowl to the radiator.

6 Remove the two bolts at either side securing the radiator top plate in place and remove from the vehicle.

7 Undo the clamp and remove the engine-to-radiator bottom hose. A lot of coolant will escape on removal of these pipes – so beware and make sure you have something in place to catch the liquid. Either retain the coolant to refill later or dispose of correctly if you intend on renewing the anti-freeze. Do NOT empty down a drain or water course.

8 Next undo the clamp and remove the radiator to header tank pipe.

9 The bottom radiator hose branches off to the header tank so remove this pipe now as well.

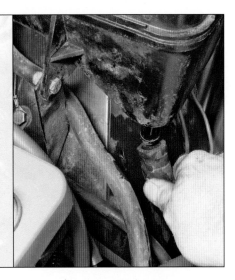

10 Remove the upper and lower oil cooler engine-to-radiator pipes and then plug all holes to keep dirt out. On automatic models remove the transmission oil cooler pipes also.

11 Lift the radiator from the vehicle and stand it in a container to allow the coolant and oil to drain from it. Dispose of the fluids correctly.

12 Once drained, place the radiator on a clean flat surface, and recover the O-rings from the oil cooler pipes.

13 Fit the top plate and the fan cowling to the radiator, this way you can see where to fit the fan without it fouling the plastic surround.

14 There are four ties that need to be threaded through the pre-fabricated holes in the fan, followed by a washer.

15 The ties are then pushed through the fins in the radiator, taking care not to damage the water veins that run vertically through the radiator. Turn the radiator over and slip the PVC tubing over the end of the tie.

16 Cut the tubing to provide a spacer through the radiator.

17 Place the protective tubing over the end of the tie and position it so that it protects the inside of the radiator where the tie passes through.

18 Fit the second washer followed by the one-use nut.

19 Use a spanner to hold the nut in place whilst the tie is pulled tight.

20 Cut away the excess tie and repeat the process from step 15 onwards for the remaining three ties.

21 With the fan unit strapped in place to the radiator, refit the whole assembly to the vehicle.

22 Refit the O-rings to the oil cooler pipes.

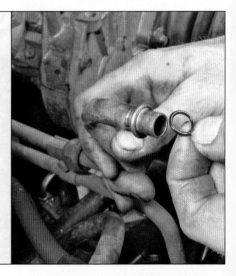

23 Now refit all the remaining pipes that were disconnected in order to remove the radiator, except for the top radiator hose – do not refit this one yet.

24 You may find it necessary to trim some of the fan cowling away in order to refit it properly.

25 The copper bulb is inserted into the top radiator hose stub. On the side of the stub we have mounted the protector (arrowed), which the bulb's pipe must be fed through to protect it. When this has been done refit the top hose as normal.

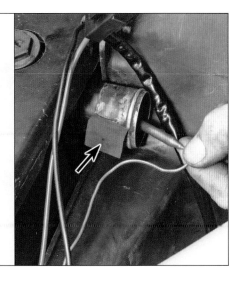

Hint: Instead of a 'copper bulb' there is also an electronic sender unit mounted inside a plastic housing available on the market today. Cut the top hose in half and remove a small length from it. Insert the housing and secure with clamps. This method is more accurate amd less likely to leak. It is more akin to a conventional car electric fan sender unit.

26 Plug the wiring connector from the separate section of loom supplied in the kit to the wiring connector coming from the rear of the fan. Mount the wiring connectors to the fan cowling to secure it away from moving parts.

27 Part of this loom includes an in-line fuse assembly – ensure there is a fuse fitted and that it is in an easily accessible location.

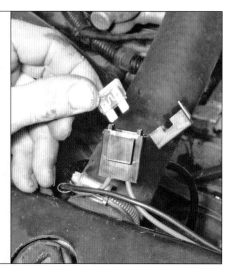

28 Mount the thermostat control to a suitable area inside the engine bay. The black control (arrowed) is how you control at what temperature the fan 'cuts-in'. Take a moment to read through the instructions so that you set the thermostat correctly and understand how the system works.

29 Refer to the wiring diagram for more information as we are fitting a switch and relay into the system, so that the fan can be switched off when wading through deep water. **Note:** *When connecting the fan into the circuit, if it is required to 'pull' air, as in our installation, connect the feed to the blue wire on the fan motor. If the fan is required as a 'blower' connect the feed to the black wire on the fan motor. The remaining wire on the motor will go to earth (in our case black).*

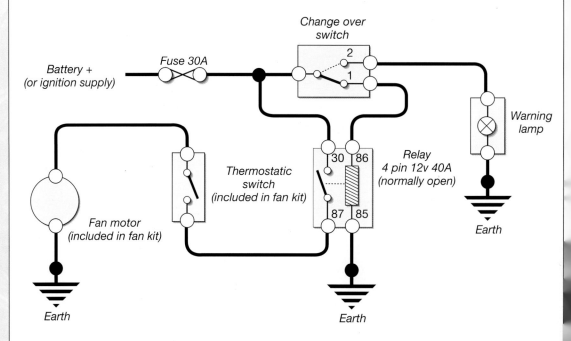

Electric fan with isolation switch (for deep water wading)

Change over switch

Battery + (or ignition supply)

Fuse 30A

Warning lamp

Relay 4 pin 12v 40A (normally open)

Thermostatic switch (included in fan kit)

Fan motor (included in fan kit)

Earth

Earth

Earth

Switch in position 1 allows normal operation of fan (controlled by thermostatic switch). Switch in position 2 will illuminate warning light and will not allow fan to cut in, even though engine coolant temperature may require it. This position must only be used temporarily when vehicle is crossing deep water. Overheating may result if not switched back to position 1 after water section has been crossed.

30 If the system is wired up directly from the battery, the fan may continue to run for a short period after the engine has been switched off (preferable), if wired from the ignition the fan will stop when the engine is turned off. So, once the circuit has been wired up according to the diagram . . .

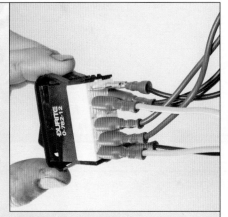

31 . . . all that's left to do is mount the switch in a suitable location near to the driver, and the installation is complete. Don't forget to refill and bleed the air from the system, checking after that the heater is hot, etc, and that everything is working fine.

Whatever type of off-roading you are into, it is a good idea to fit a snorkel to your vehicle for these reasons:

- *When crossing deep-water sections it is imperative that water does not enter the vehicle's induction system. In doing so it may travel into the cylinders of the engine and cause very expensive damage internally, usually resulting in bent con rods or worse. Water cannot be compressed in the same way as air can, so when it gets into the cylinders it commonly causes hydraulic lock and will result in major engine repairs. Fitting a snorkel will increase the vehicle's wading ability and reduce this risk of damage.*
- *Secondly, travelling along dusty tracks or plains, and especially when in convoy with other vehicles, a lot of dust is kicked up into the air. By mounting the air intake higher up the body of the vehicle, the air entering the induction system is a little cleaner, and therefore the air filter will get less clogged up and the potential for increased engine wear is also less.*
- *To complement the snorkel, a set of raised transmission breathers can be fitted to stop water being drawn into oil-filled casings when submerged in water.*

There are many different snorkel kits available on the market depending on your taste and budget. We have chosen to fit a model called Safari Snorkel, which is widely available and relatively straightforward to fit.

1 The wheel arch liner is held in place by a series of body retaining clips, these can be removed by using a suitable lever tool and the wheel arch liner lifted out from the vehicle.

2 Working inside the engine bay locate and slacken the Jubilee clip at the front of the air cleaner housing.

3 Release the two retaining clips that secure the air cleaner housing to the engine compartment . . .

4 . . . the air cleaner can now be lifted out from the engine compartment. Place on a clean flat surface as modifications to the assembly will be carried out later.

5 Tape the template supplied into position and drill a pilot hole for each of the six mounting holes.

6 Then mark the main hole and remove the template from the body.

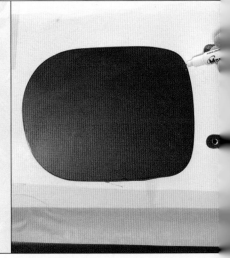

7 Apply some masking tape over the pilot holes to prevent the drill from slipping, and drill the required 16 mm mounting holes.

8 Use masking tape in the same way as above around the main hole, drill a series of pilot holes that will allow a blade access to cut the hole.

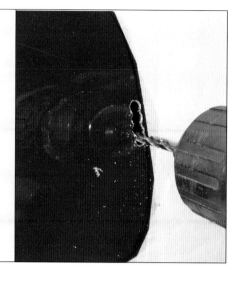

9 Using a suitable cutting tool such as a hacksaw or jigsaw, cut the hole.

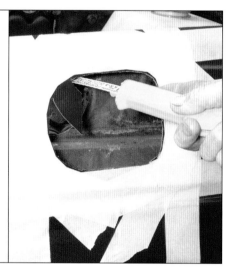

10 It will be necessary to deburr all of the holes to remove any sharp edges.

11 All bare metal surfaces must be protected by paint to stop body corrosion.

12 Next remove the self-tapping screw from the bonnet channel on top of the wing.

13 Screw the stainless steel studs into the front and centre insert positions on the snorkel.

14 Then bolt the upper mounting bracket to the snorkel body.

15 Position the snorkel on the vehicle. An assistant may be required to hold the assembly in place whilst completing the next step.

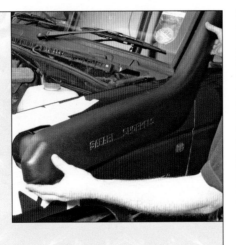

16 Drill five 4 mm holes and secure the upper mounting bracket in place using pop rivets. Remember to ensure the nuts adjacent to the pop rivets are tightened on this bracket as well.

17 Looking up from inside the wheel arch towards the engine compartment you can see where the threaded studs poke through the wing. Using the washers and nuts supplied, clamp the body of the snorkel in place. This is a fairly awkward exercise as access is very limited.

18 Moving back to the air cleaner, it is necessary to remove the air filter element from the casing to prevent any dirt/swarf entering the filter during the next step.

19 Mark and cut 20 mm off the air cleaner snout using a suitable tool. Remember to deburr the rough edges afterwards with a file.

20 Using the rubber seal provided, cut the correct length and place it around the lid of the air cleaner. Then refit the filter and seal the join to make it completely watertight using silicone sealant.

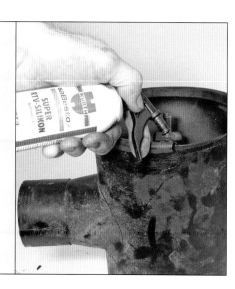

21 Back to the engine compart-ment next to place the correct size Jubilee clip on the snorkel snout. Followed by a generous layer of silicone sealant applied to the snout to seal the join.

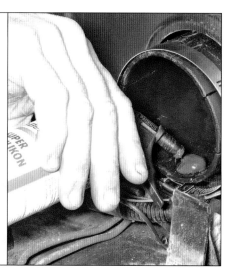

22 Lift the air cleaner back into place on the vehicle and tighten the Jubilee clips present on the snorkel snout and the side of the air cleaner housing. Remember to refit the two retaining clips at this time.

23 Shorten the self-tapping screw until there is no danger of it contacting the snorkel assembly. Refit the wheel arch liner at this time too.

24 Finally place the black Jubilee clip onto the snorkel, followed by the ram air assembly, and tighten the clamp.

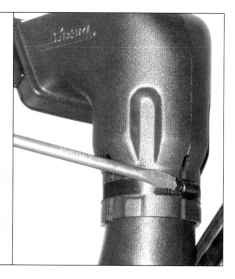

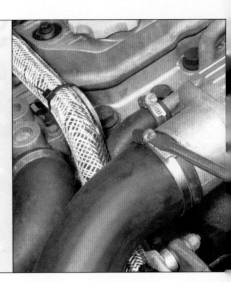

1 Locate the flexible hose from the intercooler to manifold and remove the Jubilee clamps at each end that secure the hose in place.

Silicone hoses

When upgrading your intercooler, fitment of some silicone hoses certainly complements the new set-up nicely. They are not made of traditional rubber (like the standard hoses) and last longer. The main advantage is that, as the turbo is pushing high volumes of air through them they expand less than rubber versions, therefore reducing the pressure loss in the hose and ultimately the volume of air entering the cylinders. They are readily available to order from Twisted Performance and other suppliers, come in a variety of different colours for you to choose from and brighten up the engine bay nicely.

Hiclones

When replacing the hoses you have the opportunity to fit something called a Hiclone at the same time.

The Hiclone is a stainless steel device which sits inside the air induction system. It causes turbulence in the incoming air and this turbulence is claimed by the makers to promote more complete combustion, giving more power, better fuel consumption and smoother running.

Opinion is divided about whether this device actually works. Sceptics will say that if it were any good the manufacturer would have fitted it as standard in the first place. But there is no doubt that some users claim to have experienced the benefits promised by the manufacturer.

We really can't say whether the Hiclone improved our engine's performance. We put so much extra weight on the vehicle with all the other accessories that there could be no meaningful 'before' and 'after' comparison. It's for you to decide if it's worth trying, bearing in mind that (at the time of writing at least) you can get your money back within 30 days if you're not satisfied.

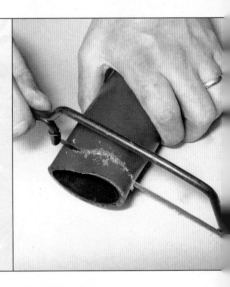

4 Due to the pipe being a little too long we had to mark the area and trim off the excess length.

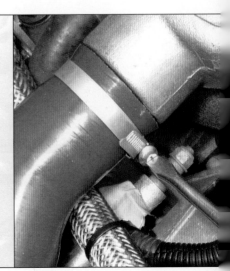

7 Place the two Jubilee clamps over the pipe and fit the hose in place permanently, tightening the clamps fully.

2 Pull the hose from the stubs and lift away from the vehicle.

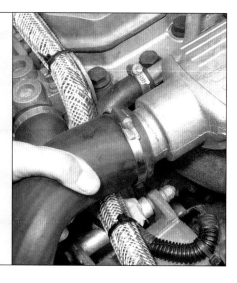

3 Offer the replacement hose into position and check for any fitment issues.

5 Offer the pipe back into place and check for fitment, then remove it one more time from the vehicle. If like us you are fitting a Hiclone to the hose this is the time to do it. Start by using a little bit of

washing up liquid to lubricate the inside of the pipe to aid insertion. If a Hiclone is not being fitted move to step 7.

6 The Hiclone is labelled with an arrow and should be fitted in the same direction as the air flows into the engine. The Hiclone may have sharp edges so watch your fingers when fitting it to the

hose. Pinch the middle of the Hiclone and insert it into the pipe pushing it down far enough, so that when the pipe is refitted it will not foul on the stubs.

8 Here the two procedures branch off. A second Hiclone will be fitted in exactly the same way as above to the flexible hose from the air cleaner-to-turbocharger . . .

9 . . . whilst the lower turbo outlet pipe is replaced with silicone one instead. Same process as before, loosening the clamps and removing the pipework from the car. Replacing the originals with the silicone pipes, refitting the pipes and tightening the clamps.

Intercooler and silicone turbo pipes

Intercoolers

A diesel engine, such as a TDi, relies on a plentiful supply of dense, cool air to aid the combustion process with the fuel. On a turbocharged engine, the spinning turbo increases the airflow into the engine but in doing so, when compressing the air, heat is generated as the molecules are pushed tightly together. Air, like most things, expands when warm, but warm air is less dense and does not have the same burning characteristics as cool air, so the compressed air is fed through the intercooler. As the vehicle moves along the road, air flows through the front grille and passes through the cooling fins on the intercooler. The induction air leaves the intercooler ready to enter the inlet manifold compressed and cooled. When the air enters the combustion chamber in the engine, it is burnt with the correct quantity of fuel to provide a noticeable increase in power. If more power is required a modified or larger intercooler may be fitted. The theory behind this modification is that the replacement unit will have a greater surface area of fins exposed so a greater quantity of induction air will be cooled to a lower temperature, which means the air entering the cylinders will be cooler and denser, and therefore will produce more power.

There are certain aspects to consider when contemplating this modification:

- *Make sure that your engine is in good condition to begin with. An intercooler will put a certain amount of additional load on the engine due to the increased amount of air under compression in the cylinders, so make sure it's up to it.*

- *It is a good idea, especially if fitting a larger intercooler, that the fuel delivery setting on the injection pump is increased slightly to compensate for this. The additional volume of air under compression can tend to make the combustion process lean, therefore producing more heat/stress. To ensure longevity of the engine we suggest you book your vehicle in with a diesel tuning specialist who is experienced in this field and can make correct adjustments so that the engine runs cleanly and reliably afterwards.*

Silicone hoses

When upgrading your intercooler, fitment of some silicone hoses certainly complement the new set up. They are not made of traditional rubber (like the standard hoses) and last longer. The main advantage is that as the turbo is pushing high volumes of air through them, they expand less than rubber versions, therefore reducing the pressure loss in the hose and ultimately the volume of air entering the cylinders. They come in a variety of different colours for you to choose from and brighten up the engine bay nicely.

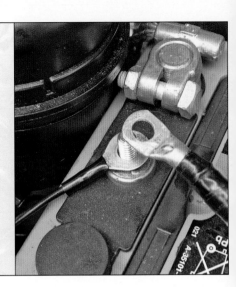

1 Disconnect the battery negative lead. You may find it easier to remove the viscous coupled fan for improved access (see *Electric fan* for more information) but this is entirely optional.

2 Loosen and remove the clips securing the two hoses (upper and lower) to the intercooler and carefully pull the hoses from the stubs on the intercooler. **Note:** *You may encounter some oil residue as the pipes are released so have a cloth to hand just in case. If there is a lot of oil present it suggests that the seals on the turbocharger have deteriorated and may require further investigation and work to fix. In an ideal world nothing should be present in these pipes. Clean the pipework using a suitable solvent to remove any trace of oil if replacement pipes are not being fitted.*

3 Unscrew the two nuts and washers (on some models clips will be present instead of nuts) that secure the cooling fan cowl to the radiator.

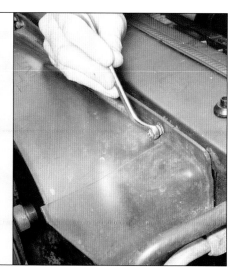

4 Move the cowl upwards to disengage it from the lower securing body clips. Once free move the cowl towards the rear of the vehicle and over the fan blades (if the fan has not been removed) to remove it completely from the vehicle.

5 Remove the four bolts (two at each end) securing the radiator top cover and withdraw it from the vehicle.

6 Carefully push the radiator forwards so that it is possible to disengage the intercooler from the support frame and lift it up and out of the vehicle.

7 Alongside our new improved performance intercooler we shall be fitting some new silicone hoses.

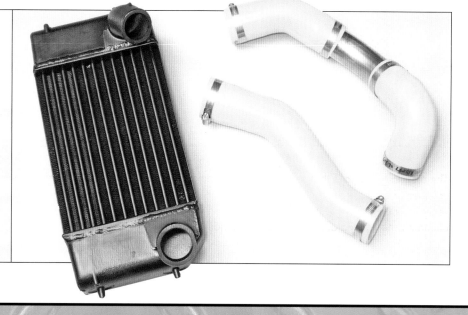

8 Offer the new intercooler into place and check the fitment. Ensure the lower lugs locate properly in their holes on the lower panel.

9 The only issue we had with ours was that the upper hose stub fouled the radiator top cover, so part of the top cover had to be trimmed to accommodate the stub.

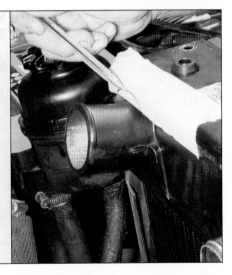

10 Once you are satisfied that the radiator top cover fits well, refit it and tighten the retaining bolts. Then refit the fan cowling and viscous fan (if removed) in the same way as it was removed.

11 Finally, all that's left to do is fit the new pipework in place of the original ones and ensure that the retaining clips are done up tightly to prevent any air leaks in the system. **Note:** *Later TDIs are fitted with an exhaust gas recirculation (EGR) valve as part of the exhaust emission control system. This valve can become clogged up with carbon and stick open, causing a loss of turbo boost pressure. The correct response to this is to clean or renew the valve - see your Haynes manual for details. It is possible to remove the valve completely and fit a blanking plate, but this cannot be recommended because it will affect the exhaust emission levels.*

A standard Land Rover exhaust system is perfectly adequate for most applications, however some owners prefer to make modifications in this area. Some want to increase engine output/breathing, some re-route the tailpipe section to avoid damage off-road, and others, particularly those with V8 engines, modify their exhaust systems to produce a more pleasing noise under acceleration.

Off-the-shelf systems are mainly aimed at people looking to gain more horsepower and there are several companies designing and producing performance diesel exhaust systems, which actually help the engine 'breathe' more freely and more often than not, produce a nice noise under load. However it should be noted that as the exhaust system is under the vehicle it will always be susceptible to damage, particularly on extreme off-road trips. In these circumstances an expensive, flash stainless steel system is probably not a good choice as the chances are it will become damaged and useless long before it ever rusts away. Most owners into 'extreme' off-roading will design and produce their own systems tailored to their own vehicle and needs. V8 engines with performance exhausts done properly can produce the most fantastic sound, and anyone who has ever experienced this cannot deny it.

On our TDi Discovery we opted to fit a stainless steel performance system, which unlike the original, has only one silencer box fitted. The results are a better gas flow, ie, less restriction, and a more beefy sound, which was not unpleasant.

Our 200 TDi is not fitted with a catalytic converter (cat) in the exhaust. Some 300 TDi models do have cats. Aftermarket exhaust systems are available which do away with the cat, and at the time of writing it would appear that (unlike petrol engines) it is possible to remove the cat and still pass the MoT exhaust emission test. However, as with the EGR valve, we cannot recommend this because the vehicle's exhaust emissions will be greater than the manufacturer intended.

If you're fitting an exhaust system which is identical to the one you're removing, check that you have the correct parts by offering up each new pipe and box against the old ones. If you're fitting a custom made system, be prepared to make some minor alterations...

1 Firstly jack up the front and rear of the vehicle and support on axle stands.

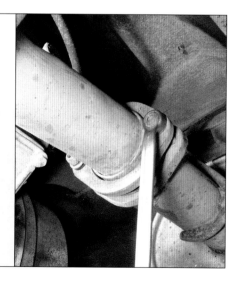

2 Unscrew the exhaust clamp nuts where the front downpipe joins the mid-box section.

3 Slide the two halves of the clamp back out of the way and, using a bar, lever the two sections of pipe apart.

4 Next remove the clamp at the opposite end of the downpipe and lift the pipe away from the car.

5 Unhook the mid-box from its rubber mountings (one at either end of the box).

6 Finally unhook the back box from its rubber mountings, making sure that the system is supported or else it will just fall onto the axle.

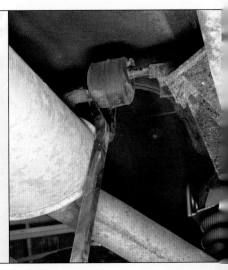

7 With the help of an assistant, withdraw the system from the rear of the vehicle and store or dispose of it properly.

8 The new exhaust is joined together using clamps that have been supplied with the system. Smear some exhaust jointing paste inside the coupling sleeves. If your system has a cat, don't use jointing paste on the engine side of it as it may cause damage - use a proper gasket.

9 Fitment of the new system is the reversal of removing the old one. Start by fitting the front downpipe in place, in our case using the original clamp as this is the only one that was not supplied in our kit.

10 Then go through the rest of the system hanging the pipes loosely in the correct place and attaching the mid-box (where relevant) and back box onto the rubber mountings. Some lubricating spray on the rubber mountings will definitely make life easier.

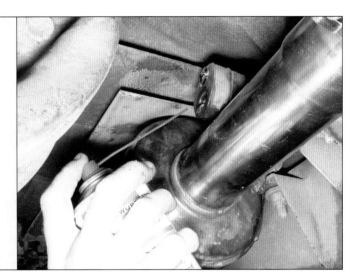

11 When the system is hanging in place and you are happy with the fitment go round and tighten all of the retaining clamps.

12 It is not unusual to find that on an aftermarket system some pipes have to be trimmed if too long. We had to make some alterations to the length of one of the pipes to ensure a proper fit; you may have to do the same.

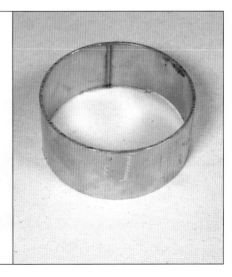

UNDERSIDE

Underbody protection and driveline

Rock sliders/jackable sills

Dan bar

Sump/steering guard

Front diff guard

Rear diff guard

Fuel tank guard

Air locker differential

Air compressor

Air line for tyre inflation

Land meter

A form of protection for your Discovery, this time to protect the sills of the vehicle. There are various manufacturers producing these and they do vary in design, but ultimately consist of a steel box section that is fitted to the sills or chassis of the vehicle, in place of the standard plastic trim panel. Their purpose, depending on design, is to protect the sill panels and lower edges of the doors from damage caused by protruding rocks and tree stumps, as once the vehicle is in contact with these obstacles the rock sliders should slide over or around them without creasing the panel work. Some designs have jacking points built in to them, which is useful if the vehicle needs side lifting rather than front or rear. Other types have longitudinal bars welded to the main bar that protrude from the vehicle. These enable the vehicle to be 'turned' around a tree if need be or can be used as side steps to assist entry/exit from the vehicle.

The bars we have chosen to fit were supplied by Bearmach and are of a simple flat finish (ie, no tree protectors or jacking points) and are attached to the chassis using strong plates. After removing the existing plastic moulding, fitment of the sliders proved quite straightforward. Due to the weight of the sliders, it is advisable to have an assistant handy.

A few days prior to installing the rock sliders it is a very good idea to apply a liberal dose of a rust preventative spray to all the fixings to ease removal. For increased accessibility under the vehicle we suggest you jack up the vehicle and support it safely using axle stands.

1 Prise away the body clips that secure the plastic kick panels to the vehicle using a flat-bladed screwdriver. Repeat the step on the other side of the vehicle.

2 The retaining nut and bolt located inside each wheel arch needs to be removed – on our vehicle the nuts simply sheared off, as they were so rusty. Support the weight of the sill because it is now free to be removed from the vehicle.

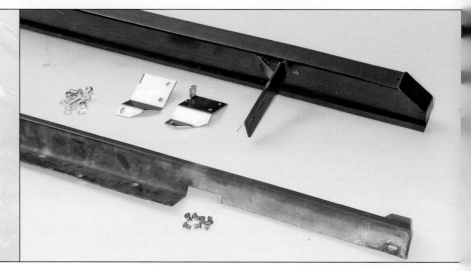

3 At this point a thorough examination of the structural condition of the outer sill can be carried out.

4 Unscrew and remove the inner carpet trim panel from inside the door.

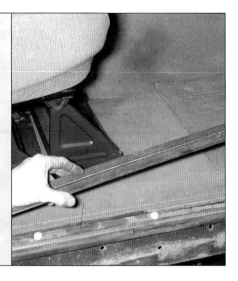

5 Lift the carpet up to reveal a rubber grommet and then lever the grommet from its hole to reveal the head of a body mounting bolt.

6 Place a socket on top of the bolt and ask an assistant to counterhold the retaining bolt whilst you complete the next step.

7 From underneath the car locate the body mounting bolt nut and remove it.

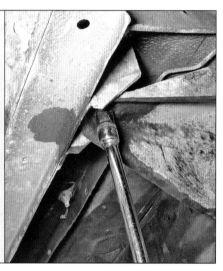

8 The rear body mounting bolt has a captive nut so removal of the carpet inside the vehicle is unnecessary. Remove the bolt, as the mounting brackets for the rock sliders will be fitted to these points.

9 The next step is to fit the brackets to the front and rear body mounting points.

10 Offer the rock slider into position and support it in place using a jack, or an assistant, whilst you bolt it to the mounting brackets.

11 It is necessary to remove some of the rubber beading around the door seals so that the rubber sits flush against the sills.

12 Use ratchet straps to pull the rock slider tight into the body in order to fully seal the rubber to the vehicle.

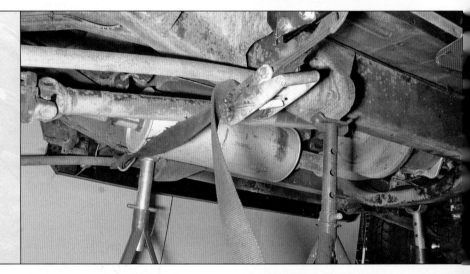

13 Once the rock slider is pulled in tight the final mounting holes in the bracket can be drilled . . .

14 . . . the nuts and bolts can be fitted and all fixings tightened. The installation is now complete.

No, you can't eat these . . . they are in fact another form of underbody protection that is available, this time for the steering rods on your Discovery. Basically they are tubular bars which are slid into place over the existing steering rods then, via a nipple, pumped with grease to provide lubrication between the rods and bars. When off-road, any obstruction that is likely to cause damage to the steering rods comes into contact with the Dan bar instead. The double thickness of a rod inside a tube becomes very difficult to bend. Don't forget to remove the grease nipple after fitment to avoid damage to it whilst off-road. They are available for both long and short steering rods and identical to fit. On our Discovery we have chosen to show the short bar fitted to the drag link.

1 Apply the handbrake, loosen the wheel nuts, and then jack up the front of the vehicle. Remove the front wheels and support on axle stands. **Note:** *You will see from the pictures, we have trolley jacks under* the axle however this is only because we were in the process of refitting the front axle at the time.

2 Undo the nearside drag link clamp bolt and the balljoint retaining nut. Remove the balljoint from the swivel housing. Use a balljoint separator if necessary.

3 Mark the balljoint, or count the number of times it takes to unscrew and remove the balljoint so that when refitting the balljoint later it will be refitted in the same location and no adjustments are required. Once the balljoint has been removed, also recover the clamp bolt. Clean the exterior surface of the drag link and apply a thin film of grease to it.

4 Using a copper hammer, gently tap the Dan bar over the drag link until it is in place.

5 Once the bar is in place, the clamp bolt can be refitted and the balljoint screwed back into drag link, observing any marks or the number of turns of the balljoint that show its relationship to the drag link. Don't forget to re-tighten the clamp and check the tightness of the balljoint retaining nut. Once completed, refit the roadwheels and lower the car to the ground.

Sump/steering guard

Another area of the Discovery that requires protection when off-roading is at the front end. Vulnerable components here are the steering rod in front of the axle (steering box drop arm to nearside swivel housing) and, to a certain extent, the engine sump. A guard can be fitted here to reduce the risk of rocks or unseen tree stumps causing damage as the vehicle travels along. Another useful feature of a steering guard is th... ...travelling through deep water sections, the flat ...uard pushes the water forward creating a bow ...vacuum in the area behind the guard ...ater being sprayed around the engine ...by spinning fan blades. ...ions of guard on the market, ...ilst others have integral ...for a hi-lift jack adapter.

Choose the type that suits your needs best. The guards are constructed from thick aluminium or steel (aluminium ones being slightly more expensive to buy, but lighter in weight) and some have holes in the guard. The ones with large, circular holes are designed to allow airflow through, which is particularly useful if the vehicle is to be used in hot climates. The downside of this is that they can get clogged up with mud easily in boggy sections. The guard we chose to fit to our Discovery comes in 3 sections, two 'blades' to be attached to the nearside and offside chassis rails, and a plate with cooling holes made from thick aluminium. The plate is secured to the blades using countersunk Allen screws for a neat finish. Fitment is straightforward, although sometimes it is easier to have an assistant nearby due to the weight of the guard when lining up bolt holes.

1 The blades mount onto the bumper retaining bolts and at a chassis point further back.
Caution: Make sure you identify the left and right-hand blades or brackets correctly.

2 Refit and tighten the retaining nuts fully.

3 Repeat the process for the other side.

4 Lift the sump guard into place and align the holes to those found in the brackets.

5 Fit the Allen screws and nuts and tighten fully.

6 Now that installation is complete the protective film can be removed from the guard and the task is completed.

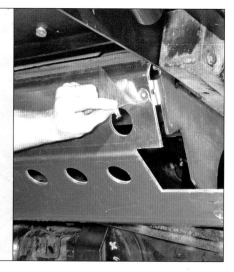

Diff guards

The main purpose of fitting diff guards is to protect the vulnerable diff pan, which is made of relatively thin material, from being damaged by protruding rocks, tree roots or similar. If the diff pan is hit hard enough it could result in two major problems – firstly it may be punctured causing a loss of lubricating oil and failure of the diff itself. Secondly the crown wheel of the diff runs very close to the inside of the pan so if dented inwards it may cause the pan to touch the teeth on the crown wheel, eventually wearing through the metal and resulting in a loss of oil and extensive damage to the diff itself.

Given that there are different styles of diff guards we'll show you how to fit two of the most popular types.

Front diff guard

As we said above, there are many different styles, but the one shown here incorporates a pan protector plate (leaving access to filler and drain plugs) and also a slider plate which protects the underside of the casing around the differential unit as well. This offers the greatest protection to the diff.

Note: *The kit supplied by Bearmach includes parts that are necessary to fit the diff guard to Discovery 2s as well as the 1 Series, so do not be alarmed if you have parts remaining after installing the guard.*

1 Jack the vehicle up and support on axle stands to improve access to the underside of the vehicle.

2 Undo the nuts securing the steering damper in place and drop both ends down.

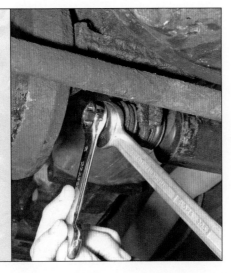

3 Supporting the weight, undo and remove the two bolts securing the vibration damper to the underside of the diff. This bracket will not be refitted later on, so discard it now.

4 Undo the two nuts at the top of the diff housing and place the top diff guard plate over the diff and secure with the two nuts.

5 Loosely fit the main body of the diff guard in place using the nuts and bolts provided. Threadlock applied to the threads of the bolts is also advisable.

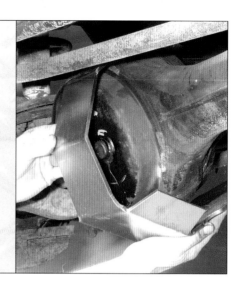

6 When you are satisfied with the fit tighten the retaining nuts.

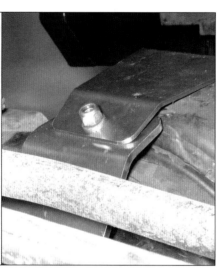

7 Using the new built-in bracket on the diff guard, refit the vibration damper and refit that end of the steering damper to the bracket.

8 Then refit the other end of the steering damper.

9 As we said earlier there are some parts that are not refitted and some are in the kit that are not applicable when fitting the guard to a Discovery 1 such as ours, so don't be alarmed if you have some parts leftover after installation.

Rear diff guard

1 Offer the guard into place checking for sound fitment and that it doesn't foul the brake lines that run nearby.

2 Using a socket and Allen key tighten the two retaining nuts sufficiently to secure the guard in place on the axle.

3 Finally make sure that you are still able to check the oil level in the diff by removing the level plug with the guard in place. If not, slightly reposition the guard.

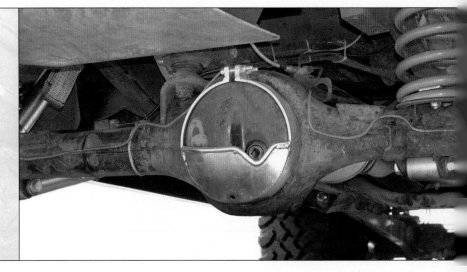

One form of protection for your Discovery that is of particular importance if you take your vehicle off-road is a guard bolted to the chassis to protect your fuel tank from damage. The fuel tank is located at the rear of the vehicle in between the two chassis rails, is made of plastic and supported/protected by a thin steel pressing. When off-roading you may find that the steel cover is not sufficient to protect the tank from damage and that something more substantial is required. If your vehicle is fitted with a tow bar this will go some way to protecting the tank but a heavy-duty steel or alloy guard which encompasses the whole area is preferred.

Several variations of guard are available. Some manufacturers offer guards with integral mounts for a

detachable tow bar such as the Southdown Guard, which is a neat solution and removing the tow bar increases the departure angle of the vehicle, thus lessening the risk of becoming stuck. However, for those of you who wish to retain the standard towing bracket, Scorpion Racing produce a guard that fits in place between the chassis rails protecting the tank but retaining the existing towing equipment.

Before fitting this piece of equipment, it would be a good idea beforehand to spray all fixings with a penetrating oil to aid removal of the bolts as it is likely they will be fairly well rusted in place, having seen all manner of debris over the years. Also, run the fuel level down to a minimum as you will be releasing the tank securing bolts and a light tank will be far easier to move about than a full one.

1 Jack the vehicle up and support on axle stands to improve access to the underside of the vehicle.

2 Undo, then remove the nuts and bolts securing the rear anti-roll bar (if fitted) to the brackets (one either side), and lower the bar.

3 Apply another liberal dose of a penetrating oil spray, then remove the nut and bolt that attach the tow bar support bracket to the chassis. Repeat this process on the other side.

4 Beware: removing the bolts from the tow bar support brackets is not an easy job due to rust build-up over the years.

5 Slightly easier to remove is the one bolt either side that secures each support arm to the main tow bar bracket.

6 Use a good strong length of bar and feed it through the holes on the anti-roll bar bracket in order to 'wedge' the fuel tank in place, because this is the time where we shall be undoing the front two tank retaining bolts. Without this bar or an assistant holding the tank in place after you have completed the next step there is the danger that the tank will fall out of the vehicle, damaging itself, pipework or wiring.

7 Remove the final two tank retaining bolts and recover the existing fuel tank guard. Before you leave the vehicle, ensure that the bar is holding the tank in place and if necessary use some additional chocks of wood to wedge the tank firmly in place.

8 Place the existing fuel tank guard inside the new heavy-duty guard. Due to the excessive weight of this piece we found it easier to put the whole assembly on a trolley jack and wheel that under the vehicle, raising the jack until the guard was in position, rather than lifting it. If you do not have access to a trolley jack we certainly advise you to ask an assistant to help you rather than attempting the job alone.

9 As the jack completes its task, it is now easy to secure the tank in place using the new bolts and captive nuts supplied in the kit. The new guard will use the existing fuel tank mounting points so put the captive nut into place . . .

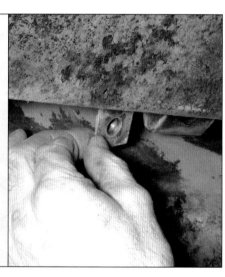

10 . . . then fit the bolts. Do not fully tighten at this stage.

11 Fit the front two tank retaining nuts and bolts then tighten them fully. You can then remove the supporting bar and/or chocks of wood, as there is no danger of the tank falling to the ground now.

12 Fully tighten the two rear tank retaining bolts then refit the anti-roll bar to its brackets. Refit the tow bar support brackets. **Note:** *It may be necessary to cut a section from the supports if they foul on the new tank guard. On both sides our support bars had to be modified in order to fit the profile of the tank guard.*

Air locker differential

Many people believe that if you have four-wheel-drive you can go anywhere, but this is not necessarily true. Under normal conditions power is sent to the wheels with the least amount of traction when the going gets tough. This happens simply because a standard differential is designed to allow each wheel to turn independently of the other, enabling the vehicle to go round corners. The downside to this is that on slippery ground a standard differential will direct all power to the spinning wheels and therefore traction is lost. If you can afford to, fit a differential lock onto the axle so that, when it is engaged, the wheels can no longer turn at different speeds to each other, instead the drive is fed equally to both wheels thus enabling traction to be regained.

The ARB air locker differential is highly rated by those in the know. We're fitting it to the rear axle here, which is what most people do if they're just having the one. Serious off-road enthusiasts will fit them to both axles, as mentioned later.

Note: *This is a lengthy procedure requiring some skill and a well-stocked toolbox. Read it through before you start and make sure you have everything required; read the instructions with the kit as well. Remember that once you've started, your vehicle will be immobile until the installation is complete.*

1 Some manufacturers recommend that the vehicle is secured on a chassis hoist to allow for a more convenient working area, whilst ensuring the wheels and axles are free to be rotated and removed. If this equipment is not available, jack the vehicle up and use axle stands to support the chassis instead. Once supported, release the handbrake and leave vehicle in neutral.

2 Clean the area around the rear differential drain plug to prevent debris entering the diff, remove the plug using a suitable key and fully drain the oil. **Note:** *Any metal particles in the oil may indicate a worn component.*

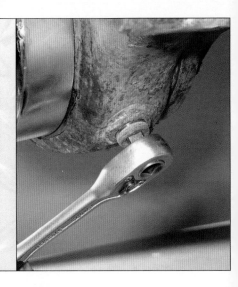

3 Undo and remove the five bolts and washers that secure the halfshafts to the centres of the hubs and withdraw the shafts. Recover the gasket from the halfshaft flanges, renew as necessary.

4 Make some alignment marks so that the prop is not unbalanced when refitted, then undo and remove the four nuts and bolts that hold the rear prop shaft to the diff.

5 Next, undo and remove the ten retaining nuts on the differential housing. **Note:** *Two of these nuts hold the rear brake pipe bracket in place. Position it carefully out of the way so that the pipes are not under any stress.*

6 Before lifting the differential away from the axle, retrieve the two washers from the brake pipe bracket studs. The differential can then be lifted off the studs, away from the vehicle and placed on a clean flat surface.

7 Prior to stripping the diff it is essential that the bearing caps are marked in such a way that you will be able to distinguish the left- and right-hand sides, and also orientation, upon refitting. Bearing caps must NOT be interchanged. Punch marks to the bearing caps followed by similar marks on the differential housing is an easy way of remembering which side is which.

8 The backlash on the crown wheel (also known as the ring gear) must now be measured using a DTI (dial test indicator). Set the DTI on one of the ring gear teeth and zero it. Hold the pinion flange still and rock the ring gear back and forth; note the variation in the DTI reading. This is the backlash. Rotate the ring gear 90 degrees and take another reading. Land Rover state that the backlash should be between 0.10 and 0.17 mm, but you may find that yours is outside those limits.
Note: *A backlash measurement outside the specified range is not necessarily a cause for worry. If the diff was not noisy and there is no evidence of abnormal wear you should aim to have the same backlash on reassembly as you found here.*

9 Next tap the adjuster nut locking pins outward from the centre of the bearing caps until they are flush with the bearing bore surface . . .

10 . . . and remove the locking finger.

11 The bearing cap bolts (2 each side) can now be loosened.

12 Land Rover recommends a special service tool (LRT-54-508) for removing the two bearing adjuster nuts, however a homemade tool can be fabricated easily. Retain the left-hand nut as it

will be required on refitting and label appropriately so it does not get mixed up. Use a new nut for the right-hand side.

13 The bearing caps may require some gentle persuasion with a copper mallet to free up before removal . . .

14 . . . once loose, they can be removed from the assembly and stored in a safe place.

15 Lift the differential carrier assembly from the housing. This is an excellent opportunity to check the condition of the pinion bearing by rotating the prop shaft flange and feeling for roughness or play. Renew as necessary.

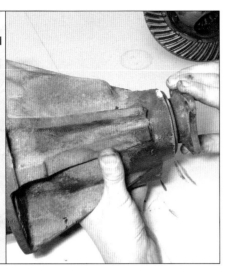

16 Remove the tapered carrier bearings from the unit, ensuring you keep the bearings and race matched.

17 There are several ways that the carrier bearings can be removed, for example by using a bearing puller or a hammer and punch. Once the bearings are removed and paired up with their correct outer races they can be checked for wear and renewed as necessary. It is essential that the left- and right-hand side carrier bearings and races are refitted as removed so label/store them appropriately.

18 Using a vice to hold the unit in place, remove the ten bolts that secure the ring gear.

19 Gently tap in a circle around the ring gear with a copper hammer to separate it from the carrier assembly.

20 Clean any locking compound and dirt from the ring gear bolts, bolt holes and mating faces. It may be necessary to re-tap some of the threads if they are showing signs of becoming stripped. Remove debris from the bolt holes.

21 Then clean the air locker flange and remove any cable ties or other packaging that may be present. **Note:** *A thin layer of high-pressure grease applied to the ring gear shoulder of the air locker will help prevent parts seizing.*

22 With the aid of a hot air gun or similar method, heat the ring gear to slightly expand it so that it will locate onto the air locker assembly easily. Do not heat the ring in excess of 100°C. If hot water is used to heat the ring gear, ensure that it is dried completely.

Caution: When heated, do not handle the ring gear with bare hands as it will burn the skin easily and, due to the thickness of the metal, the ring will retain that heat for a long time.

23 Using suitable tools or protective gloves lift the ring gear onto the air locker assembly, ensuring the bolt holes are aligned.

24 Temporarily insert one bolt (arrowed) to keep the bolt holes aligned, then gently tap the ring gear into place with a copper mallet. Don't use bolts to pull the gear home – you could strip the threads.

25 Apply thread lock to the ring gear bolts. Insert the bolts and tighten them in a criss-cross sequence to 58 Nm (43 lbf ft). You'll need to have someone hold the assembly still, or secure it in a vice with soft jaws.

26 Refit the carrier bearings. A film of high pressure grease applied to the bearing journals will facilitate this. It is imperative that the left- and right-hand sides are refitted as removed. Gentle use of a hammer and punch is acceptable if access to a press is not possible.

27 A hole measuring 11.2 mm (7/16") must now be drilled through the differential for the air line. Mark an area on the right-hand side (opposite the ring gear side) that is clear of the differential unit and other moving parts as the air line must not be obstructed in any way.

28 Secure the diff housing in a vice. When drilling it is essential that you seal off the inside the housing to protect the pinion area using a cloth or, as we have done, a magnet – this will catch the majority of metal filings generated from drilling.

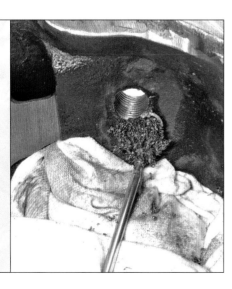

29 Tap the hole from the outside using a 1/4" NPT (National Pipe Taper) thread tap. Then remove any sharp edges and metal filings that may have fallen into the housing.

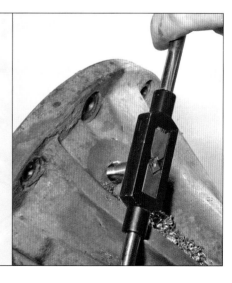

30 Place the air locker into the housing and refit the bearing caps. It is imperative that they are refitted on the same side as they were removed (look for the punch marks). Insert the bearing cap retaining bolts and hand tighten.

31 Prior to installing the adjuster nuts ensure that the threads on the inside of the bearing caps and differential housing are perfectly aligned, if not, threads can be stripped when attempting to fit the adjuster nuts.

32 Setting the backlash on the diff can be time-consuming. First screw the original left-hand adjuster nut and tighten until all backlash between the ring and pinion gears is eliminated, then back it off 90 degrees (one quarter turn). Do not adjust again, as this nut sets the backlash. **Note:** *Clearance must exist between the side of the bearing cap and air locker. If not the cap must be removed and filed until clearance exists.*

33 Screw a new adjuster nut into place on the right-hand side until you get a backlash reading on the DTI of between 0.10 and 0.17mm, or the figure measured during dismantling. This may require you to tighten the nut quite tight until you achieve this figure. Turn the crown wheel 90 degrees and measure the backlash again.

34 Once the correct backlash has been set, insert, tighten and torque the bearing cap bolts to 90 Nm (66 lbf ft). Then recheck the backlash at different points around the crown wheel.

35 Oil the O-rings supplied and fit into the grooves on the inner edge of the seal housing. When inserting the O-rings ensure they are not twisted when seated in the grooves as this will lead to premature wear and leaks.

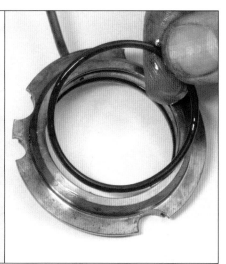

36 Lubricate the seal housing running surface of the air locker generously with oil . . .

37 . . . and slide the seal housing into place on the bearing journal with a gentle twisting motion until it is flat against the adjuster nut. The gently twisting motion allows the O-rings to be moved into place on the journal without becoming twisted.

38 Rotate the seal housing until one of the two large cut-outs line up with the locking finger. You may find that the locking finger has to be filed so it does not contact the air locker oil seal housing as this must be free to float.

39 Refit the locking pin to secure the finger in place.

40 Install the spring clip by firstly hooking both ends of the clip into the small aligned cut-outs on the seal housing and adjuster nut . . .

41 . . . then gently levering the clip into the groove of the seal housing using a small screwdriver. The seal housing should now be prevented from rotating and still sitting flat against the adjuster nut.

42 Apply thread sealant to the bulkhead body. Then screw the body into the tapped hole on the diff housing and tighten. Wipe away any excess thread sealant on either side of the housing.

43 Using your hands, gently bend the seal housing tube to the required profile on the outside of the seal housing, ensuring that you allow enough length for the tube to protrude from the bulkhead fitting on the diff housing. **Note:** *The seal housing must be allowed to freely float and self-centre on the bearing journal after the tube is connected to the bulkhead fitting, so make absolute sure the tube is not under any tension and that it is not pulling on the seal housing. The tube must not interfere with the bearing caps, air locker or ring gear either.*

44 Once the tube has been bent to the correct profile, mark the pipe and cut using an automotive brake line cutter. Never use a hacksaw or any other cutting tool as they will leave metal filings in the air system.

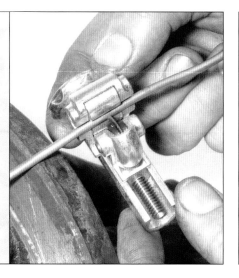

45 Insert the trimmed tube into the bulkhead fitting and you should be left with something that looks like this.

46 Place the O-ring over the seal housing tube protruding out of the bulkhead fitting.

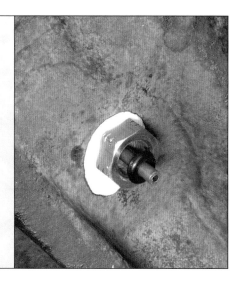

47 Then insert the small, drilled end of the centre compression nut (the thread has been partially relieved on the bulkhead end of the compression nut to identify its orientation) over the housing tube, screw it into the bulkhead fitting and lightly tighten.

48 You may bench test the air locker at this point. If clean compressed air is applied to the seal housing tube, the air locker should now engage. If you suspect an air leak firstly check the O-rings for damage. If the leak persists, disassemble the bulkhead fitting and use soapy water to test that, then clean all threads and re-apply thread sealant. Once you are satisfied that the air locker works correctly, place a dust cap over the end of the centre compression nut to prevent any dust or dirt entering the air line.

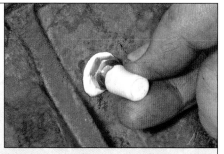

49 Renew the paper gasket on the axle housing flange, then reinstall the differential and refit the parts removed at the start of this operation. Refitting is a reversal of removal.

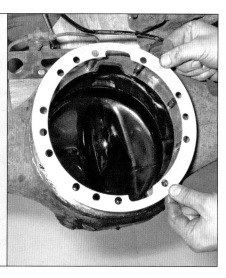

Air compressor

ARB recommend that you use their air locker and air compressor together, although you should be able to use an alternative source of air to lock the diff(s) if you wish. There are a few things that you need to check with your supplier before using a different compressor, such as:

- The air supply will match the size of the air port on the air locker solenoid.
- The air supply must match the pressure requirements.
- The tank capacity must be enough to actuate two air lockers in one charge so that no hesitation is felt when locking two differentials.
- The air supplied must be clean – free of water, rust, dirt and other debris.
- We fitted a single air locker to the rear differential, so check your kit for instructions on what to do if an additional diff locker is being fitted.

1 Remove one of the plugs from its port in the compressor tank. Select the double-threaded nipple, apply some thread sealant, then insert into the port and tighten. Then apply some more thread sealant to the free end of the nipple.

2 Screw the second single-thread nipple into the inlet side of the solenoid stamped with a 1. The air line will be secured to the orange push-in fitting on the opposite end of that nipple.

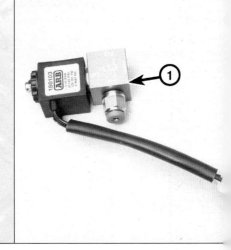

3 Next assemble the solenoid on the side marked with a 2 to the compression tank. Position the assembly in an upright position so that it does not obstruct any other ports on the tank.

4 Screw the pressure switch into position in the centre port on the tank.

5 Find a suitable area in the engine bay for mounting the compressor. Then using the mounting plate as a guide, mark the four holes and drill.

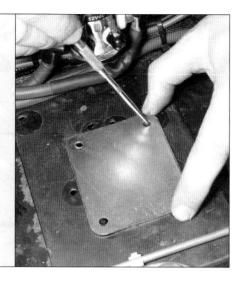

6 Assemble the compressor into place using the fixings provided in the kit. With the line in place the compressor retaining clamp can be tightened.

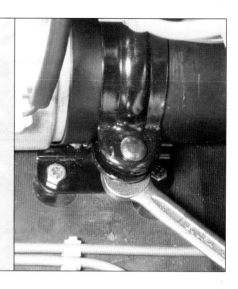

7 The loom that is supplied with the compressor comes in two sections. The first part is wired up inside the engine bay then passed through the bulkhead. As the wiring enters the cabin, the smaller part of the loom is then attached to these wires.

Differential lock

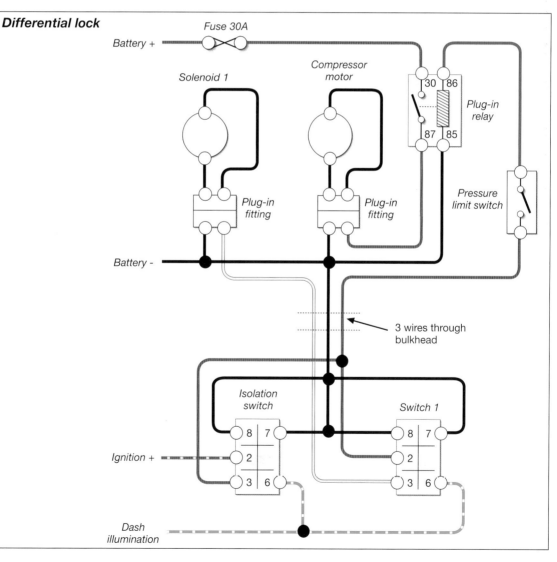

8 Mount the relay in a suitable place inside the engine bay using a self-tapping screw. There is a wiring plug in the loom that connects to the relay so locate it and push into place.

9 Drill a hole in the bulkhead large enough to pass wires through. Remember to fit a grommet to the hole.

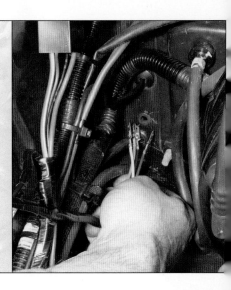

10 Locate the red and blue wires with separate connector plugs on the ends and fix them to the terminals on the pressure switch.

11 The black and yellow wires with a connector plug from the loom are now connected to the wiring plug from the solenoid.

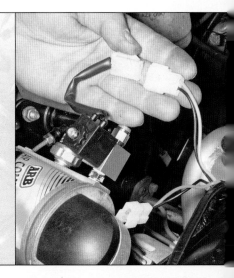

12 The red and black wires in the loom are then mated to the red and black wires from the compressor.

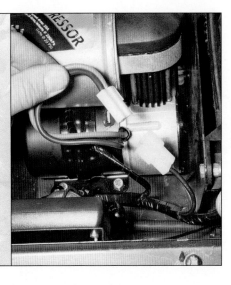

13 The wiring plug that houses the green and black wires is not required unless you have fitted a second air locker, in which case this would be connected to the second solenoid. If you have only fitted one air locker, tape up the connector and cable tie it to the loom out of the way.

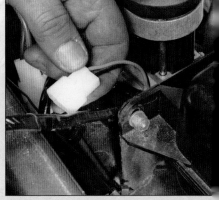

14 Move back inside the cabin now and pick up the wiring that was routed through the bulkhead. The wires must now be assembled to the spare plug provided in the kit

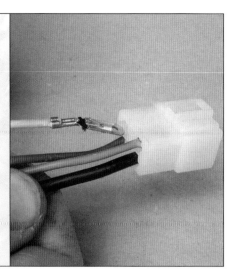

15 The second section of loom is now joined to the first by connecting the wiring plugs – one from the second section of loom and the other from the plug you have just wired up.

16 Run the wiring for the switches behind the trim to the area in the cabin where you are mounting the switches. At this time it is a good idea to make up a mounting plate for the switches. They must be located within reach of the driver, in a position where they will not be accidentally operated by a passenger or vulnerable to contact with water. Select the switch labelled 'compressor' and fix the wiring labelled 'isolation switch' on the loom, to the rear of that switch.

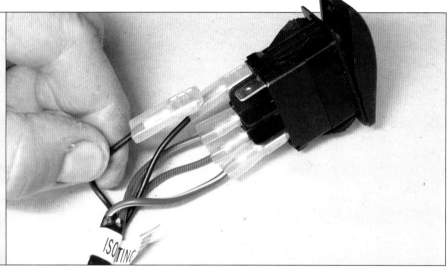

17 Similar to the last step, select the switch labelled 'rear air locker' and fix the wiring from the loom labelled 'switch 1' to that. Again, if you are not fitting a second diff locker the 'front air locker switch' and 'switch 2' wiring on the loom can be taped up and ignored. **Note:** *Make sure the face of the switch is the right way round as the faces are designed to be very difficult to remove.*

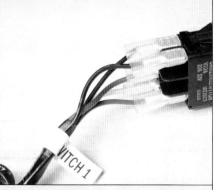

18 The final two wires from the loom must now be routed toward the rear of the fusebox. The blue/white wire is spliced into a sidelight illumination whilst the red/yellow wire splices into an ignition feed.

19 Move back to the engine bay now and, starting at the compressor, trim the end of the pipe squarely using a sharp blade, then fix it to the push-in fitting of the solenoid by inserting the line fully into the fitting. Using your fingers pull outwards on the flange of the fitting, ensuring the line is still fully inserted, then gently pull outwards on the air line until you feel it clamped in place. To remove the air line pull outwards on the flange whilst pushing the line into the fitting as far as possible and holding it there. Then push inwards on the flange and pull the air line out of the fitting.

20 The rest of the air line can then be routed under the vehicle towards the differential. Do not trim the air line until you are sure you have enough to reach the diff without any unnecessary excess. Depending on where you are routing the wire under the vehicle consider the following points:

- *Leave enough slack on the air line to account for full suspension travel.*
- *Do not leave lengths of cable hanging under the vehicle, as they may become tangled on debris.*
- *Ensure the line is not routed near any sharp edges that may pierce it.*
- *The air line must run free of kinks or restrictions.*
- *The line must not come into contact with any hot surfaces, as it will melt if subjected to extreme heat.*
- *Support the line with cable ties.*

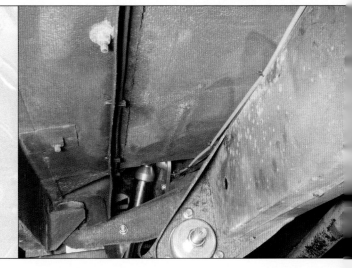

21 As the line reaches the differential, assemble the bulkhead fitting which comprises the air line, support tube, ferrule, outer compression nut and support spring. Insert the tube fully into the centre compression nut on the diff housing. Screw the outer compression nut into place and tighten. Finally assemble the support spring over the outside of the outer compression nut.

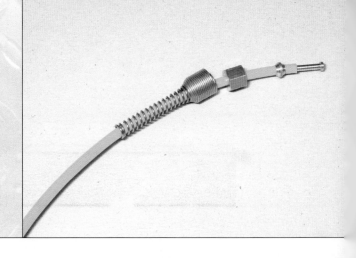

22 Now that all the work to the differential has been completed the last job here is to refill the oil.

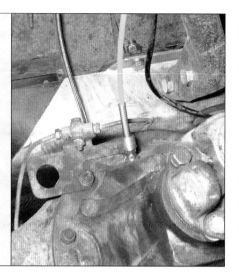

23 Last but not least, return to the engine bay once more and connect the remaining red and black wire to the live and earth terminals respectively. Take the time to read through the operating instructions supplied in the kit and the test procedure before you refit the roadwheels and lower the vehicle to the ground.

Air line for tyre inflation

It is possible to purchase a kit that will give you an additional air line from the compressor. This may prove particularly useful for people who are travelling off-road over varying terrain – softer terrain such as sand where tyres have to be deflated, and harder surfaces where tyres will need to be re-inflated With our 33" tyres, foot pumps take a lot of effort and time to fill the tyre again, so an air line eliminates all this effort and gets you moving again.

1 Disconnect the two connectors from the pressure switch and remove the switch entirely from the port on the compressor. Apply some PTFE tape to the threads on the T-piece and insert that into the port formerly occupied by the pressure switch. Apply more tape to the threads of the air chuck and screw that into place on the T-piece using two spanners to secure it in place.

2 Using more tape applied to the threads of the pressure switch, screw that into the port on the top of the T-piece and reconnect the two wire connectors.

3 Screw the push-in fitting to the free end of the air line – this plugs into the air chuck. The other end of the line already has an adapter on it, to fit the Schrader valve on the tyre. The air line can remain in the engine bay, away from hot or moving parts, to be removed when required to inflate the tyres.

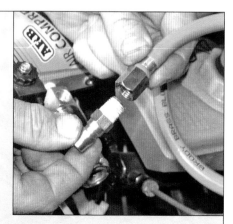

Land Meter aka clinometer or pitch 'n' roll meter

A Land Meter will only tell you what angle the vehicle is currently at, not the angle in front or behind you, and is in truth really only a gadget that should not be relied on for safe off-road driving. In many cases off-road vehicles have been modified and are usually loaded heavily on the roof rack so Land Rover's figures for approach/departure angles and, more importantly, roll-over limits are all changed anyway. Remember this gadget will not read the ground ahead and if the vehicle is modified it will only give you a very limited amount of information you can use on your trips off-road.

1 Find a place to mount the meter so that it will be visible to both the driver and front passenger. It must be mounted horizontally on a flat surface. Ensure that both dials are indicating zero when the vehicle is stationary on flat ground.

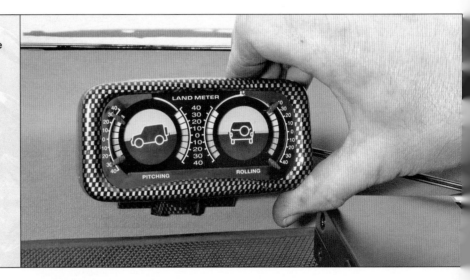

2 There are 2 options for mounting the Land Meter: the first being an adhesive pad. If you choose this method, ensure you thoroughly clean the area on the dash using a suitable degreaser before sticking the unit in place.

3 The second option, and one that we favour, is to use two self-tapping screws.

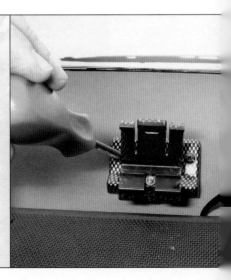

4 Next remove the lower steering column trim. Then find a way to route the twin cable from the meter, under the dash.

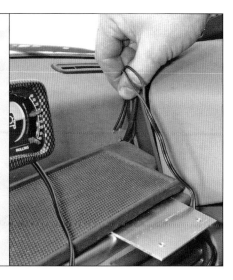

5 Once the cable is under the dash the wires can be separated. One of the two wires will go to a good earth point on the body or the battery.

6 The second wire will be spliced into a feed that becomes live when the sidelights are switched on, providing illumination to the dials for night-time driving. The wire to the bulb at the rear of the cigarette lighter will provide this feed perfectly.

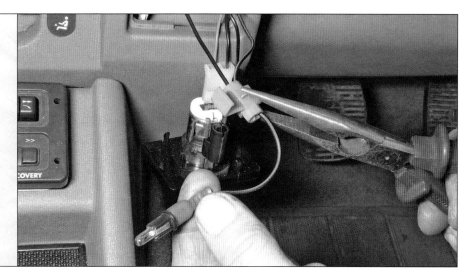

7 Test that the meter illuminates before refitting the cigarette lighter and the steering column lower trim.

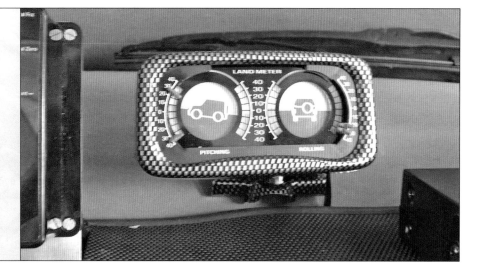

SUSPENSION

Multi-shocks

Front suspension

Extended brake lines

Rear suspension

Rear dislocation cones

Bush renewal

Air cylinder installation

The shock absorber's job is to dampen the action of the suspension, preventing the body and wheels from bouncing uncontrollably as they travel over surfaces that aren't perfectly smooth.

A typical shock absorber is constructed of a sealed tube with a rod and piston protruding down inside. The tube contains oil and the piston has valving and orifices through which the oil is forced as the suspension travels through its range of motion. This converts the oscillations of the springs into heat, reducing unwanted compression and rebound cycles of the suspension. Shock absorbers play no part in supporting the weight of the vehicle.

Conventional oil-filled shock absorbers can suffer from foaming of the oil when they have to work too hard. The result is a lag in damping. To combat this, gas-filled shock absorbers are available. These shocks are similar to non-gas-filled units

in construction, but contain an additional piston, behind which is a nitrogen-filled chamber. The force exerted on the shock absorber's oil chamber by the nitrogen-charged piston prevents the shock oil from aerating.

Most vehicles are equipped with one shock absorber per wheel, and this is usually adequate. Vehicles used off-road sometimes need more than one shock per wheel. This is because a single shock just isn't capable of converting all of the violent suspension action into heat. Multiple shock setups also look really cool! Kits are available that allow you to convert your single-shock setup into a multiple shock-per-wheel rig. The most common type is a front dual-shock kit that uses an aftermarket upper shock mount, or hoop, that bolts to the frame and the existing upper mount.

Whenever lowering or raising your vehicle, be sure to match the shock absorbers to the travel of the new suspension. Even though the standard length shock absorber can be compressed and will fit between its mounts, it will be very close to being bottomed-out and will limit the travel of the suspension. Solution? Shorter shock absorbers. Obviously, on a raised vehicle longer shocks will be needed.

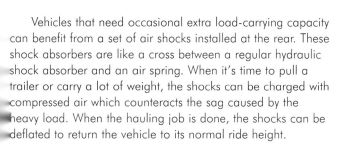

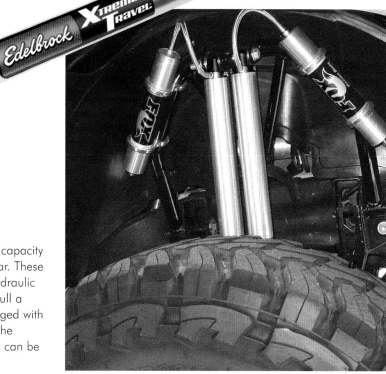

Vehicles that need occasional extra load-carrying capacity can benefit from a set of air shocks installed at the rear. These shock absorbers are like a cross between a regular hydraulic shock absorber and an air spring. When it's time to pull a trailer or carry a lot of weight, the shocks can be charged with compressed air which counteracts the sag caused by the heavy load. When the hauling job is done, the shocks can be deflated to return the vehicle to its normal ride height.

Front suspension

Choosing the correct type of springs and shock absorbers is paramount to ensuring you get the best out of your vehicle. With so many spring choices on the market, think very carefully about what you intend using the vehicle for. For instance, does it carry very heavy loads? Do you use the vehicle for towing a heavy trailer? Do you travel at motorway speeds a lot of the time or is the vehicle purely for recreational use? These questions are very important, as a 2″ lifted vehicle is not very stable at high speeds, particularly if you have to make a sudden lane change for example. Also take into consideration what tyre size you use or intend to use, as raising a vehicle by fitting longer springs can enable fitment of some larger rubber which looks nice. Alternatively if you only use your Discovery for fast road work you might consider a −1″ spring set and thicker anti-roll bars for increased stability through corners.

What we are trying to say is that your suspension system is personal to you and your Discovery, so choose carefully after looking at all the options.

On this particular vehicle we have chosen to demonstrate a full suspension kit that will give extreme axle articulation over rough ground (remember, wheels touching the ground will give traction) and that would lift the vehicle high enough to fit 33″ mud terrain tyres (with modifications to the arches!). A different front prop shaft had to be fitted to the vehicle after its 2″ raise, so enquire about this possible extra purchase when ordering your kit.

The kit being fitted here is the Scorpion Racing Extreme Kit, which is very comprehensive. Rather than fit the factory metalastic bushes, polybushes will be fitted instead to complement the new set up – the originals are well past their sell-by date now!

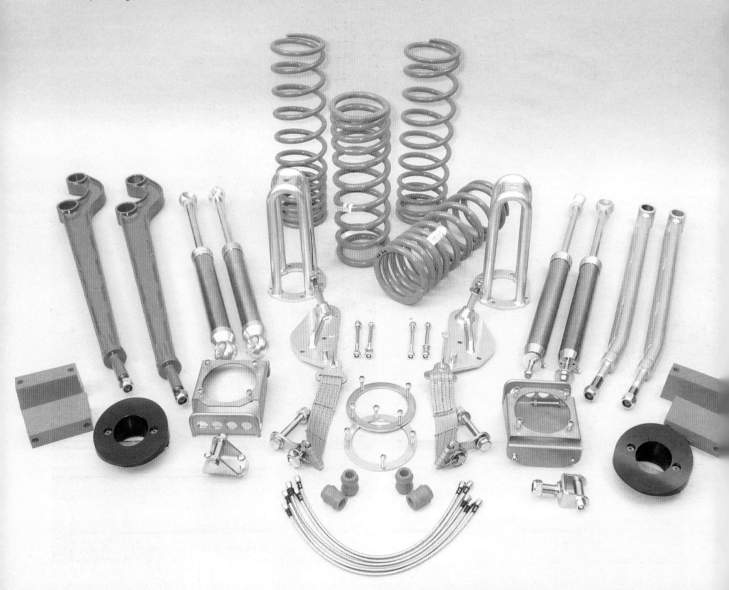

Front shock absorber and spring removal

Note: *24 hours before commencing fitment, apply a liberal dose of a penetrating oil spray to all nuts and fixings so that it will ease the removal of those that have rusted into place.*

1 Apply the handbrake, and loosen the front roadwheel nuts. Then jack the front of the vehicle up and support the chassis on axle stands. Remove both front wheels.

2 Position a pair of jacks under the front axle and raise until they are supporting the weight of the axle fully.

3 From the engine bay, locate and loosen then remove the four retaining nuts securing the shock absorber turret to the upper spring mount.

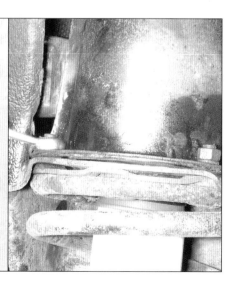

4 In order to gain better access to two of the four nuts and washers that secure the shock absorber turret to the chassis you may find it necessary to remove any pipes that are in the way.

5 Finally slacken and remove the shock absorber lower mounting nut. A pair of large grips may be required here to stop the shock from turning while undoing this nut.

6 The shock and turret assembly can now be lifted out of the vehicle. The lower washer and mounting rubber must be retained should you wish to re-use the shocks in the future.

7 Lower the jacks, but do not let the weight of the axle stretch the flexible brake pipes at either end.

8 Before removing the spring it may be necessary to fit some spring compressor clamps. The coil spring can be lifted away from the vehicle and the turret retaining bolt ring recovered.

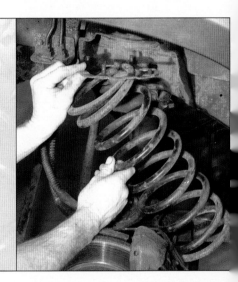

9 Remove the lower spring seat held in place on the axle by two retaining bolts and washers. If the Extreme kit is not being fitted and a simple spring and shock replacement is under way, it may be necessary to clean up the lower spring seat and refit it to the axle. Check your kit to see if a new spring seat has been supplied.

Extended brake lines

Whenever a lift kit is installed, you need to make sure your brake lines are still long enough to accommodate the full distance the suspension is capable of travelling – not just when the vehicle is standing at ride height. They may reach the calipers okay with the vehicle sitting there, but when the suspension rebounds what's going to happen?

Anything more than a minor lift will require longer brake lines. So, as long as you have to change them, you might as well go with a set of braided stainless-steel lines. They're tough and will give you better brake response (less prone to 'ballooning').

Fitting the Scorpion Extreme Kit

Warning: This procedure requires at least two people to be carried out safely.

Note: 24 hours before commencing fitment, apply a liberal dose of a penetrating oil spray to all retaining nuts and bolts so that it will ease the removal of those that have rusted into place. It'll take you a while to unpack and check the list of components so leave yourself plenty of time to carry out this job – it can be done by any competent mechanic.

1 Apply the handbrake, and loosen the front roadwheel nuts. Then jack the front of the vehicle up and support the chassis on axle stands. Remove both front wheels.

2 Visible here from the engine bay, yet only accessible from underneath the car, slacken and remove the prop shaft-to-differential retaining nuts and bolts. Then remove the prop-to-transfer box flange bolts and remove the propshaft.

3 Position two hydraulic jacks under the axle and raise until the jacks are supporting the weight of the axle.

4 Unscrew the nut securing the radius arm to the chassis and remove the washer and outer mounting bush. Repeat the procedure for the other side.

5 Slacken and remove the nuts and pivot bolts securing the Panhard rod to the chassis and axle and remove the rod from underneath the vehicle.

6 Disconnect the drag link balljoint from the swivel pin housing and the anti-roll bar connecting links, if fitted, from the axle. The anti-roll bar will not be refitted afterwards.

7 Remove the shock absorbers and springs as described previously.

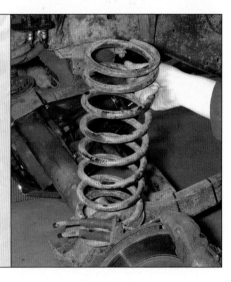

8 Disconnect the axle breather hose from the chassis. Do not pull the axle forwards just yet – only lower it sufficiently.

9 In an ideal world this is the point at which you undo the union nut and clamp the flexible brake pipe to prevent fluid loss, so that the brake pipes leading up to the bracket are free to move away from the vehicle with the axle. However, our nuts were rusted so tight into place that the pipes had to be cut and then clamped. That has just caused an extra few quid's worth of bother so be aware that you may face the same problem! **Note:** *On models with ABS trace the wiring back from each wheel sensor and disconnect it from the main wiring connectors. Then work back along the wiring freeing it from any clips so that the cable is safely removed with the axle.*

10 Now, with the help of an assistant supporting the radius arms, lower the jacks so that the axle moves away from the chassis, ensuring that everything is disconnected. Then wheel the jacks out from under the vehicle. Go back now and remove the old rubber bump stops and plates from the vehicle.

11 Never leave the axle supported by the jacks alone – replace each jack with an axle stand.

12 Now remove the radius arm retaining bolts. This may prove harder than it sounds as on our vehicle they had seized solid inside the bushes. No amount of gentle persuasion would remove them so in the end they had to be cut and the remains punched out. The old arms may be discarded as new castor-corrected arms are supplied in this kit.
Note: *Retain the large metal washer from behind the foremost bush.*

13 Here comes the exciting part – the first component from the kit can be fitted! We start with the lower shock absorber brackets that are bolted into place on the original spring seat. This is an ideal time for that seat to get a little TLC by having a wire brush down and a fresh coat of paint.

14 Each of the castor-corrected arms must now have their polybushes pushed into place. The two halves of the bush are pushed into the arm, then the steel insert is pushed through the bush. Obviously the fitment of a Polybush kit is optional, there are other makes but we think these are pretty hard to beat in terms of price and quality.

15 When this task has been completed the arms can be bolted back into place on the axle. But only after a liberal dose of copper grease has been applied to the bolts.

16 It's also a good time now to cable tie that axle breather hose to the nearside castor arm as this will prevent it from becoming entangled on the refitment of the axle.

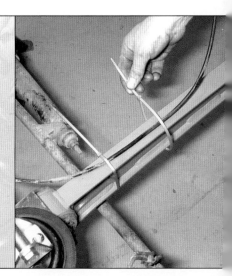

17 To the engine bay we go now, armed with the template supplied in the kit and a drill. Place the template onto the upper spring seat with the longest straight-edged side facing the engine. Make sure that the holes marked with an A align with the existing holes for the original turrets.

18 Next drill four 8 mm holes in the positions marked B on the template. After drilling ensure the rough edges are filed off. Check the new upper turret retaining ring threads align with these newly drilled holes, as some adjustment may be required.

19 Working on a clean flat surface, the two polybush bump stops can be built-up on their corresponding metal plates . . .

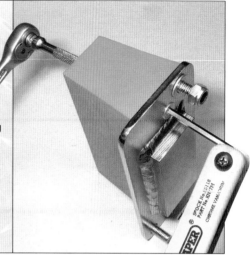

20 . . . followed by swift and certain fitment to the vehicle. Then fit the old large metal washer we kept back earlier to the end of the radius arms followed by one half of the polybush, and copper grease the threads.

21 It's now time to refit the axle, so swap back the axle stands for jacks and with the aid of an assistant wheel the assembly back into place.

22 Fit the coil spring and upper turret retaining ring into place and then raise the jack until the retainer locates through the holes you drilled earlier, held in place by the spring.

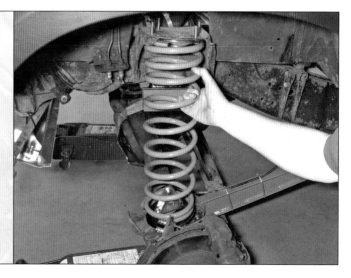

23 Fit the corresponding remaining halves of the polybushes to the castor arms and using the Nyloc nut provided secure the arm in place.

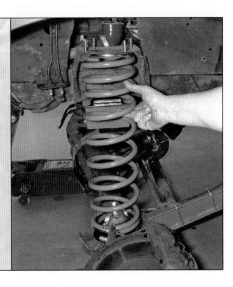

24 Using a vice, gently press the lower shock absorber bush into place, remembering to protect the metal from the jaws of the vice. Lubricating spray will help no end here too.

25 On a clean flat surface, bolt the shock absorber to the new turret. Fit one rubber bush then pass the stud through the turret. Fit the second rubber bush followed by one steel washer, before securing the whole assembly with the self-locking nut.

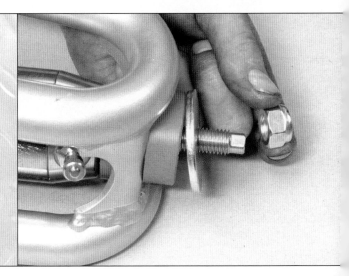

26 Pass the shock assembly through the inner wing and spring, then hand-tighten the turret retaining nuts.

27 Using some lubricating spray push the metal tube supplied into the polybush.

28 Insert the lower shock absorber retaining bolt and tighten the nut.

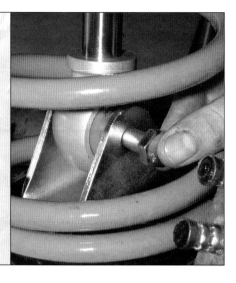

29 The upper shock retaining nut must now be tightened. All bolts will need to be checked, tightened and torqued when the wheels are refitted and the vehicle lowered to the ground.

30 Refit in the reversal of removal: Panhard rod, track rod balljoints and drag link from the swivel pin housing.

31 Fit the front flexible brake hoses to the vehicle now.

32 If like us you had to cut the brake pipes earlier it will be necessary to replace these with new. Once the rear suspension has been fitted (because you may have to cut the pipes on the back too) it will be necessary to bleed the brake system.

Rear suspension

When changing the suspension on the rear of our Discovery we found it easier to remove the rear axle complete from under the vehicle, build up the new components and then refit it as a complete unit. Bear in mind, we were changing the rear trailing arms for non standard items and also replacing the brake lines. If you are only changing the springs and shock absorbers then axle removal is not necessary as these items can be replaced *in situ*. Refer to the Haynes workshop manual for more information on this procedure.

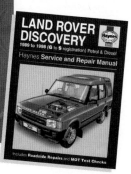

Rear axle removal

1 Loosen the rear wheel nuts, chock the front wheels, then jack up the rear of the vehicle and support with axle stands. Remove the rear wheels.

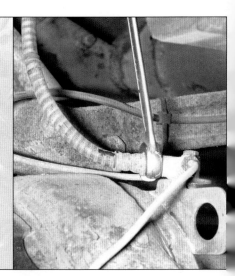

2 Trace the brake pipes back from the calipers to their union piece situated at the top of the axle. Slacken the union nut and disconnect the pipe. Remove the retaining clips and release the pipe from the axle.

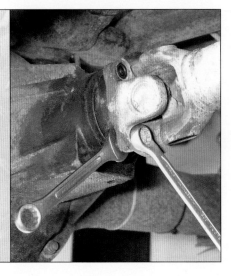

3 Counterhold the bolts, and unscrew the nuts securing the rear prop shaft to the differential flange.

4 Disconnect the axle breather from the vehicle body.

5 Position a hydraulic jack under each side of the axle and raise it until it is supporting the weight of the axle. Then undo the bolts securing the trailing arms to the vehicle chassis.

6 Disconnect the shock absorbers from the axle.

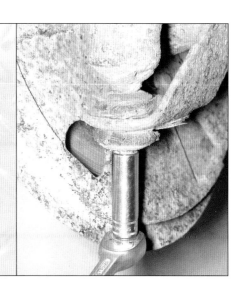

7 Remove the A-frame balljoint from the axle, then lower the jacks and, with the help of an assistant, roll the axle out from underneath the vehicle, taking care to lift the trailing arms so that they are not damaged on removal.

8 Undo the retaining nuts and bolts, then remove the upper shock absorber mounting plate on both sides of the vehicle.

9 Fit the new shock mounting plates in place of the old ones using the existing bolt holes. This plate also retains the straps that lock the axle in place for when you need to jack up the vehicle. The lower

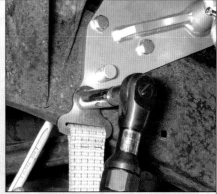

bolt retains this strap in place, so make sure the bolt is threaded through the hole in the strap then through the mounting plate. Once fitted the straps are secured in position ready for use.

10 Fit the new polybushes to the shock, then slide the shock absorber onto its upper mount and tighten the Nyloc retaining nut.

11 Unbolt and remove the old bump stops . . .

12 . . . and, in their place, build up the new bump stops onto their mounting plates and then fit to the chassis.

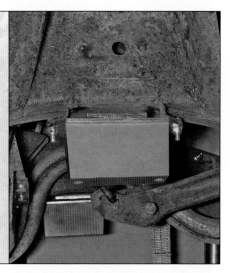

13 Using the template supplied in the kit, drill the mounting holes marked A in the old upper spring seat.

14 Next bolt the new upper spring seat into place on the chassis.

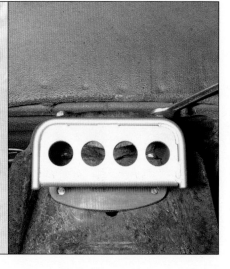

15 On a clean flat surface build-up both ends of the new trailing arms with the polybushes.

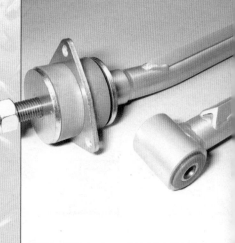

16 Return to the axle now and remove it from the jacks and support with axle stands instead. Next, unbolt the trailing arms from their axle mounting brackets.

17 Remove the spring from its lower seat and clean the area using a wire brush.

18 Mount the spring slider to the spring.

19 Bolt the new progressive springs in place, they are not directional in this set-up and we have chosen to mount them with more coils at the top; other kits might have the orientation specified by the manufacturer.

20 Fit the new flexible brake hose to the union nut at the top of the axle.

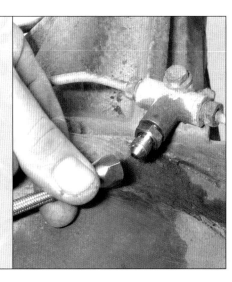

21 Bolt the trailing arms, and the brackets that secure the straps to the axle, in place on the axle mounts.

22 Using silicone sealant, apply some to the bolt holes on the spring slider. This prevents stones getting into the bolt holes and damaging the slider platform as the spring returns from its dislocated state.

23 Fit the lower mounting bracket to the shock absorber.

24 Replace the axle stands with jacks once more and roll the whole axle assembly back under the vehicle.

25 Raise the jacks so that the spring slides into position in the upper spring seat.

26 Refit the trailing arms on either side and tighten the Nyloc nuts. Tighten them to the specified torque once the wheels are refitted (see the workshop manual for tightening torques).

27 Bolt the lower shock absorber mounting to the axle. Then refit all the items that were removed for the axle to be removed – the A-frame balljoint to axle, propshaft, axle breather, and extended rear brake pipe. Remove the jacks from under the axle, refit the roadwheels, jack up the vehicle a little more to remove the axle stands and lower the vehicle to the ground. **Note:** *Once installation is complete, bleed the brakes, starting with the caliper furthest away from the master cylinder. Refer to the Haynes workshop manual for more information on this procedure. Remember to go back and tighten all the relevant nuts on the suspension and wheels to the relevant torque figure.*

LAND ROVER DISCOVERY
1989 to 1998 (G to S registration) Petrol & Diesel
Haynes Service and Repair Manual
Includes Roadside Repairs and MOT Test Checks

Dislocation cones

When travelling off-road in your Discovery over very uneven terrain it is possible to unseat the top of one or even both of the rear springs when one side of the suspension is fully compressed and the other side has drooped to its limits. As the rear springs are only retained at the bottom, there is a small chance of the top of the spring popping out. This can happen even to standard vehicles but it is less likely on ones that are fitted with anti-roll bars, as these limit axle articulation.

Dislocation cones can be fitted to allow the spring to become unseated when on full travel and then to guide the spring back into its correct position as the vehicle weight is returned onto it. They are relatively easy to fit but require the removal of the spring to do it. When changing/uprating your springs, this is a good time to carry out this extra modification.

Bush renewal

When having to remove metalastic bushes, such as those fitted to the suspension arms on a Discovery, the preferred way of removal is to use a hydraulic press as sometimes these bushes can be very stubborn to remove, particularly if they have been subject to many years of use. If a hydraulic press is not available they can be removed by using the following methods.

1 To remove a bush, for example from a trailing arm, begin by clamping the arm in a vice then, using a cutting tool such as a hacksaw with interchangeable blades, cut through the bush.

2 Alternatively, using a socket and hammer it is possible to firstly shock the bush free from the trailing arm, and then punch it out.

3 If like us you are fitting Polybushes to the trailing arm insert the two halves of the bush into the arm and then insert the metal tube that holds the pieces together – it really is that simple. If you are fitting a different make of bush it may be possible using a socket and hammer to press the bush into place. **Note:** *Using an assortment of large and small sockets and a bench mounted vice, it is possible to use the vice as a press and push the bush in or out. However, this may require a great deal of effort.*

Air cylinders are a great way to increase your load or towing capacity. They're a good choice because they can be inflated when necessary and will reduce the amount of sag in the rear of the vehicle, but when the towing or hauling job is done they can be deflated, returning the vehicle to stock kerb height and ride quality.

1 Raise the rear of the vehicle and support it securely on axle stands placed under the chassis rails (this will allow the axle to hang down with the coil springs extended). On this vehicle the rubber insulator at the top of the coil spring had to have the centre of it trimmed to make a larger opening for the stem on the air cylinder. A utility knife did the trick.

2 On some vehicles the exhaust pipe is fairly close to the rear coil spring, so we had to install the supplied heat shield. First we bent the mounting tabs into the proper angles . . .

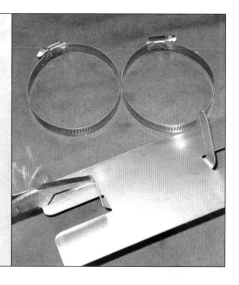

3 . . . then mounted the heat shields on the pipe and secured them with the hose clamps.

4 Push a length of air line up through the hole in the upper insulator (don't cut it yet because you don't know how long it needs to be).

5 Remove the cap from the stem on the air cylinder, roll the cylinder up from the bottom to push out as much air as possible, then reinstall the cap to keep the cylinder deflated.

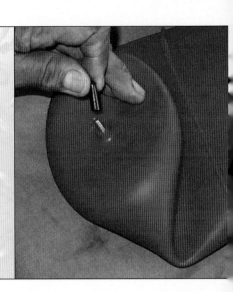

6 Work the cylinder through the coils then remove the cap; the cylinder will begin to suck air in but you might have to help it get back into shape. Be sure to follow the directions with the kit; on some vehicles the cylinder must be installed with the stem pointing up, but on others it must be pointing down.

7 Install the protector over the stem end of the cylinder . . .

8 . . . then attach the end of the hose to the stem, securing it with the hose clamp. Once you've done this, set the protector down around the stem.

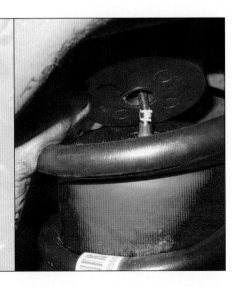

9 Find a good place to route the air lines, keeping them away from moving suspension components and hot exhaust pipes. Use the supplied T-fitting and clamps to join the two lines from the air cylinders, then secure it to the underside of the vehicle with the mounting strap and screw. The third line from the T-fitting gets routed to the Schrader valve, used for inflating the cylinders.

10 We decided a good out-of-the-way spot for the Schrader valve would be just inside the right side rear door – easy to get to, but not in an area where it could get damaged easily. So, the hole was drilled . . .

11 . . . the Schrader valve was secured to the hose and the nut, washer and insulator were placed on the valve . . .

12 . . . then the valve was passed through the hole and fastened into place with the insulator, washer, locknut and nut.

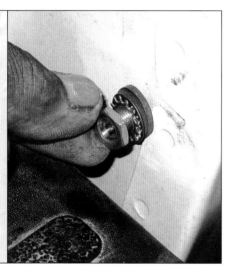

13 Our kit came with a sticker listing the minimum and maximum pressures for the system. Even when the bags aren't being used to give the back end a boost, the minimum pressure must be maintained to keep the bags inflated enough to prevent them from becoming chafed.

14 After inflating the system, you can check for leaks by spraying all of the connections with a solution of soapy water. Leaks will cause the solution to bubble.

15 That's it! The only visible part of the system is the Schrader valve, and it's pretty inconspicuous. Whenever this vehicle needs a little help out back when towing, all we have to do is open the rear door and charge the cylinders with air (keeping an eye on the maximum allowable pressure, of course).

BODYWORK

Removing wheels 'n' jacking up
Wheels and tyres
Spare wheel carrier
Rear bumper
Rear cradle and winch
Front bumper
Front winch
Weathershields
Roll cages
Nudge/roo bar
Rear step
Roof rack
Wheel arch extension kit
Custom panels
Chequer plate
Customising bonnet
Customising load areas
Bush wires
Rear ladder
Tinting windows

Removing wheels 'n' jacking up

Anyone who wishes to use their Discovery off-road should consider purchasing a hi-lift jack at the earliest opportunity. It is one of the most versatile pieces of equipment you can own as an off-roader. Apart from the obvious use of jacking up your vehicle whether to change a wheel or 'slew' the vehicle out of ruts, it can be used for pulling a load such as by winching or as a compressing tool.

Winching

The hi-lift jack makes a great winch, due to its ability to cover a reasonable distance without continually re-rigging. With a few ropes and shackles this piece of equipment can get you out of trouble. Safely attach a strong rope to the carriage or foot of the jack (the bit that goes up and down) and to a recovery point on your Discovery. Then, using a second rope attached to an anchor point (tree or ground anchor set), attach the free end to one of the steps of the hi-lift jack using a suitably rated shackle. Then when operating the jack, as the foot moves along the jack, the ropes tighten, moving your vehicle. This operation may need to be repeated several times depending on how far you need to 'winch' as the jack only has a certain amount of travel.

Jacking

If your vehicle becomes 'high-centred' in deep ruts, jacking up the vehicle using a hi-lift jack will get you out of trouble. By jacking the front wheels clear off the ground and with the help of an assistant the vehicle can be pushed sideways off the jack placing the wheels on higher ground. It may be necessary to repeat this procedure at the rear of the vehicle in order to free it completely.

The need to change a tyre may arise, and if the vehicle has long travel suspension or you are on uneven or soft ground the standard bottle jack (though very useful) is often inadequate. A hi-lift jack will raise the vehicle a lot higher, but be careful because a vehicle raised high on a jack becomes very unstable, so a great deal of care is required – practise at home on level ground first to familiarise yourself with the procedure.

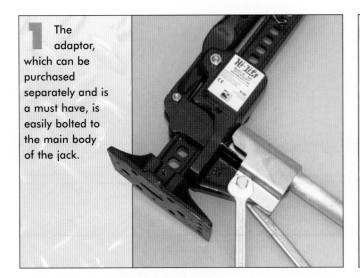

1 The adaptor, which can be purchased separately and is a must have, is easily bolted to the main body of the jack.

2 If, like us, you have fitted the Extreme suspension kit, make sure that the rear suspension straps are secured to the anchor on the axle, effectively limiting the axle travel and allowing the wheels to be lifted clear of the ground.

3 Remove the rear step (if present) as it is in the way of where the hi-lift jack will be positioned.

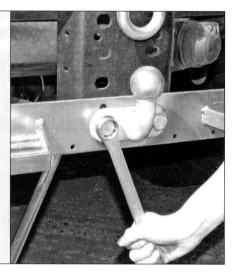

4 Chock the front wheels because the vehicle will try to roll forward when the jack is operational. Then loosen off but do not remove the roadwheel nuts.

5 Place the adapter into the slot in the bumper and begin operating the jack. As soon as the vehicle is clear of the ground the wheel can be removed and axle stands put under the axle for stability.

6 Once the vehicle has been lowered to the ground remember to release the suspension straps from the axle and refit the rear step.

7 There are many places on the vehicle you can store your hi-lift jack such as inside the vehicle or on the roof rack, but our favourite lies with a bracket available to buy from Scorpion Racing that mounts the jack to the spare wheel carrier on the rear door. Wherever you choose to store yours, ensure that it is stowed away safely yet remains accessible at all times.

Wheels and tyres

There are so many combinations of wheels and tyres that can be fitted to a Discovery it is impossible to discuss them all, so we will provide you with an overview of this topic.

Firstly, wheels – manufactured from either steel or light aluminium. Alloy wheels can really look good on a Discovery, however they are susceptible to damage and prove costly to fix. Sometimes they crack and replacement is the only cure. Steel wheels are ideal for off-road Discoveries because if they are bent they can be simply hammered roughly back into shape to get you moving again and a replacement is generally cheaper if required.

Secondly, tyres: a great deal of choice available here but sizes and tread patterns apart, there are basically three different types – Road, Mud and All-Terrain tyres.

Road tyres, as the name suggests, are largely road biased, and ideal if nearly all your excursions are black top.

All-Terrain tyres – these are slightly more aggressive than road tyres, and aimed at users that require a 50/50 balance of on and off road driving. They generally maintain good on road-handling characteristics, yet cope reasonably well in off-road conditions when needed. Ideal tread pattern for use in sandy conditions and wet grass. In summary a good all round tyre.

Mud terrain tyres, as the name implies, are mainly for off-road use in wet, muddy conditions, but also fare well on rocky terrain too. The open aggressive tread block patterns are self-cleaning and bite into soft surfaces when the going gets tough. They are designed to be an approximate 80/20 mix of off-road to on road usage. On tarmac, in the dry, they generally behave fairly well, but do generate a lot more tyre noise than other types. Watch out in wet or slippery road conditions beacuse, due to the open tread block pattern, there is less rubber touching the road surface compared to other types, which invariably means less traction. Therefore extra care is required when cornering or negotiating roundabouts whilst using these tyres.

Size is an important consideration when choosing replacement tyres for your modified Discovery. A taller tyre may look good and increase ground clearance, but you must check they will not foul the bodywork, chassis, brake pipes, etc when on full lock or axle articulation (suspension travel). Some trimming of the body panels may be required and even adjustment of the steering lock stops as well to prevent rubbing.

On our project Discovery we had already fitted a suspension lift kit, trimmed rock sliders to fit and cut away the wheel arches so that we could fit our 33" diameter mud terrain tyres. This requires a lot of work (even more if the Discovery has four doors!). The extra work does not end there, either. In theory the speedometer must be recalibrated to take account of the increased rolling circumference, otherwise it will read slow. There will also be an effect on the gearing, which can be corrected by fitting lower ratio crown wheel and pinion sets – but that will upset the speedo calibration too. You can see that fitting larger wheels than standard is not always as straightforward as it may seem and quite often further work is needed to do the job properly. It is advisable to seek advice from a Land Rover specialist before making an expensive purchase.

Spare wheel carrier

Unless you plan never to change the size or style of your wheels it will be necessary at some point to change not only the spare wheel on the rear door but also the carrier to accommodate a different-sized wheel. It is advisable to check the condition of the door hinges before you strap a 33" tyre to the rear door – our vehicle survived the proceedings well but if you have a large amount of corrosion around those areas you may find the door slumps or, in extreme cases, snaps off completely! Therefore, any corrosion must be repaired properly first. Devon 4X4 supplied our carrier and as carriers go we think it's a pretty good one.

1 To remove the outer spare wheel trim, remove the 3 nuts and washers then lift away the trim.

2 Exposed are the three wheel nuts that hold the spare wheel to the carrier, so remove these and lift the wheel from the threads.

3 With the spare wheel gone it's easy to see the 6 bolts that need to be removed in order to bin that bracket.

4 Before these bolts can be removed, the door card needs to be removed from inside the tailgate (see *Chequer plating* for more information).

5 Once the door card is removed the nuts are easily accessible and the carrier can be removed.

6 Take the new carrier and fix to the door in exactly the same way as the old one – only the profile of the bracket has changed – as the mounting holes in the new bracket align with the existing holes in the door.

7 You may require an assistant to help you with this next step – it involves lifting up the extremely heavy wheel over the threads and into place on the carrier, then securing in place using the three original retaining nuts. Not as easy at it sounds!

8 It is sensible to replace one of the carrier retaining nuts with a locking wheel nut as the spare wheel left in its current state is vulnerable to thieves. A tyre cover is another good product to fit in order to protect the rubber from UV light – speak to your wheel supplier; sourcing a 33" cover may be a problem

Rear bumper

deteriorate and the bumper bar itself, being steel, is prone to corrosion. To remedy this we have chosen to fit an aftermarket all-steel, powder coated version. There are several advantages that this modification will provide:

- *Improved cosmetic appearance.*
- *Integral hi-lift jacking points – essential if off-roading.*
- *Integral recovery point – again essential for off-road use.*
- *The opportunity to upgrade your lighting from standard 200 Series to the later 300 Series additional bumper lights.*

The bumper supplied by Scorpion Racing has been designed to improve the departure angle of the vehicle and protect the rear corners as well. It is made of all steel construction and powder coated black. It features cut-outs to fit the later 300 Series lights and comes with two red reflectors to keep you legal.

There are two positions (one either side) to use a hi-lift jack adapter, and an optional swivel eye recovery point can be purchased separately allowing recovery of your own vehicle or safe recovery of another.

Before attempting to fit any aftermarket bumper, examine the rear of the vehicle for any signs of corrosion and have it repaired properly. As recovery can generate very large forces that could be sufficient to tear the recovery point from the vehicle if not securely attached, with possibly fatal consequences.

Prior to removal of the bumper it is a good idea to spray the fixings with a penetrating oil a few days beforehand to ease removal.

Due to the rear overhang on a Discovery, whilst driving off-road the corners of the bumper become quite vulnerable to damage mainly due to the fact that they are plastic mouldings. Over the years, as found on our project vehicle, they will

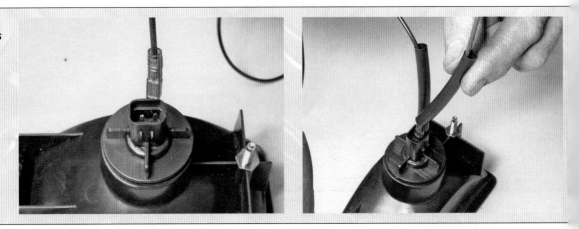

The 300 series lamps we used need unusual connectors. It is possible to use small spade-type connectors and shrink wrap tubing.

1 Remove the existing bumper. You will need an assistant to support the weight whilst the nuts and bolts securing the bumper to the chassis are removed. The tow bar must also be removed.

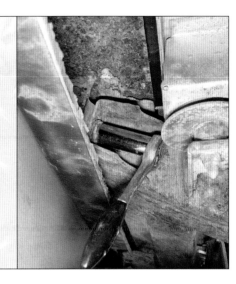

2 The reinforcement plates fit behind the original bumper chassis mountings. It is recommended that the plates are welded in place. Align the holes in the reinforcing plates with the existing mounting holes before welding.

3 If you are fitting a swivel recovery eye, place it through the C-shaped mounting bracket, then slot the bracket onto the rear crossmember so that the surface facing rearwards is vertical. Secure in place using the double captive plate and bolts.

4 With the aid of an assistant, lift the bumper into position over the protruding swivel eye if fitted – a screwdriver pushing the eye outwards from behind the bumper will help you achieve this. If the swivel eye is not being fitted, align the bumper with the four bolt holes found in the C-shaped bracket instead.

5 Once the bumper is correctly positioned, fit and hand-tighten the four central retaining bolts – the two lower retaining bolts first, followed by the upper two. Do not fully tighten yet.

6 Next fit the two socket-head bolts and nuts to the reinforced bumper-to-chassis mountings.

7 Go back and fully tighten the four central bolts and the outer two socket bolts.

8 Return to the swivel eye and, using circlip pliers, fit the circlip over the protruding end of the eye. Hold the eye still with a metal rod as shown.

9 Fit the shackle and pin into place and then fully tighten the retaining nut.

10 As mentioned earlier, we intend to upgrade the existing rear lighting by fitting the later model rear bumper lights. The 300 Series bumper lamps consist of two rear lights (inner part) and left/right indicators (outer part). These can be obtained from Land Rover parts suppliers or dealers at reasonable cost. However, we intend to fit identical lamps with clear lenses supplied by Devon 4X4. We want to fit additional rear lights to the inner section of the lamp using a coloured bulb and create a low-level working light in the outer section. This working lamp will improve visibility when reversing at night, hitching up a trailer or as a general work light. We will fit clear 21W bulbs for this purpose. They will be switched on/off using a dash-mounted switch. There is no need to fit a relay for this purpose providing that a suitable switch is sourced, as the current draw remains relatively low.

11 As you can see from the wiring diagram, the wiring is kept simple. The rear lights are connected in parallel to the existing rear light cluster – your workshop manual will tell you which colour wire to connect to. Connect the left-hand light to the left-hand body lamp and similarly on the right hand side. Doing this will not overload any existing lighting circuit on the vehicle and, normally, the standard vehicle fuse will not need uprating. If you don't want to fit work lamps, alternatively connect the indicators in the bumper lamps to the existing left and right indicator wiring in the rear light clusters. **Note:** *This may activate the trailer warning lamp on your dash when the indicators are operated as the relay senses an extra load in the circuit just as if you were towing. If this is the case ask your local Land Rover*

dealer to supply you with the correct flasher relay to prevent this, but still operate correctly with a trailer attached, as this is a legal requirement. This is fitted in the dash on the driver's side just above the pedals.

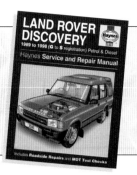

Rear bumper mounted low level work lights

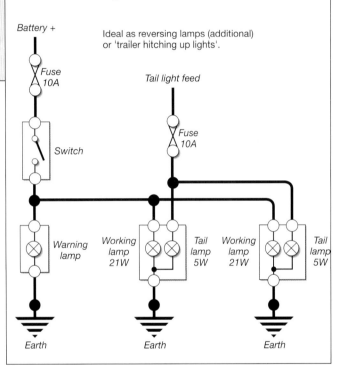

Battery +

Fuse 10A

Switch

Ideal as reversing lamps (additional) or 'trailer hitching up lights'.

Tail light feed

Fuse 10A

Warning lamp

Working lamp 21W

Tail lamp 5W

Working lamp 21W

Tail lamp 5W

Earth   Earth   Earth

12 Once the lamps are all wired up, use a hot melt glue gun or silicone sealant on the connections to provide a good waterproof seal at the rear of the lights.

13 Bolt the lights into the rear bumper and screw in the protective grilles.

14 The final job is to go back and ensure all wires are routed safely out of sight and that the switch is securely mounted in a sensible location inside the cab.

Rear cradle and winch

When you are driving off-road and find yourself stuck, normally the easiest way of becoming unstuck is going back the way you came. Sometimes this is not possible and winch extraction is required, perhaps by the closest vehicle behind you. Assuming you are on your own and forward progress is not an option, using a rear winch is one way you are likely to be able to recover yourself.

On a Discovery it is a complex job to fit a permanently mounted rear winch and would normally involve some serious modification to the vehicle unless you opt, as we have, for a removable cradle to hold the winch. The cradle, supplied by Bearmach, was easily modified to fit a trailer tow hitch to it, so that the complete unit would fit onto a standard 50 mm ball

hitch. This has the advantage of being able to swivel in-line with the pull.

To take care of the electrics, we fitted heavy duty battery cables to the rear of the vehicle terminating in an Anderson plug. These grey connectors are available through Durite and most motor factors and are sometimes referred to as 'fork lift' type plugs. They enable safe and easy connection and disconnection of heavy duty electrical cables from the battery. The ends of the cables are soldered into metal terminals, then fitted into one half of the plastic plug. The winch cables are then fitted with their terminals in the same way and into the other half of the plug, thus enabling the two halves to be plugged together for use, unplugged and unhitched and the complete unit stored away after use.

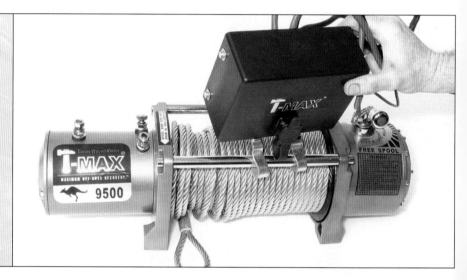

1 Your first job is to assemble the winch and wire the control box to the winch motor. Begin by securing the control box to the bracket on the main body of the winch.

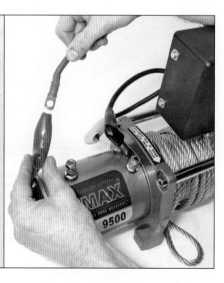

2 On the back of the control box there is an assortment of wires. Three of these are colour-coded and of similar length – red, black and yellow cables complete with colour-coded protective sleeves . . .

3 . . . these cables must be bolted to the corresponding colour-coded terminals on the winch motor. Smear some petroleum jelly on these connections after they have been made, prior to covering with the protective boot.

4 The longer black cable, complete with ring terminal, is then connected to the underside of the winch motor.

5 Bolt the winch to the cradle. As it is portable and will be stored in the load area for most of the time, anti-theft bolts aren't a necessity. If you are fitting a rear bumper with built-in cradle, anti-theft bolts are a must.

6 Fit the cable guard to the front of the winch cradle, ensuring the retaining nuts are fully tightened.

7 The live and earth cables that remain are going to be fitted with large terminals that plug into an Anderson plug. The connections must be soldered.

8 With both terminals fitted to the ends of the cable they can be slotted into the plug. Once the connection has been made the wires are very difficult to remove.

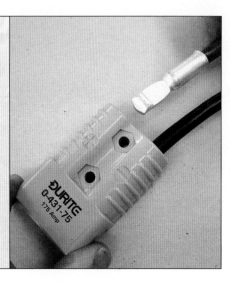

9 Bolt the handle to the plug. This handle aids quick, fuss-free removal of the plug when the winch is disconnected from the tow ball mounting.

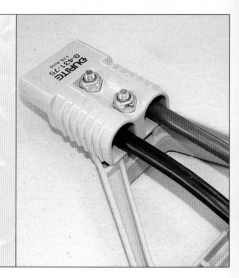

10 If not already done, disconnect the battery earth lead(s). Connect the positive feed cable to the battery (or auxiliary battery). Because the winch draws a very high current (up to 400 amps) and the cable has to go from one end of the vehicle to the other, you need to use heavy cable to avoid an unacceptable voltage drop. Starter motor cable is about right. In exactly the same way as earlier, connect the cable to the plug by soldering the terminal in place.

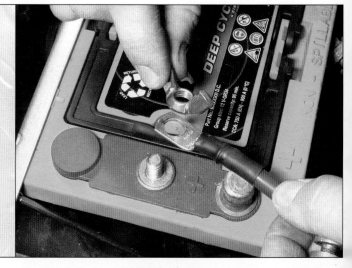

11 As close as possible to the battery, fit a suitable fusible link in the cable – refer to the manufacturer's specifications for the rating of the fuse.

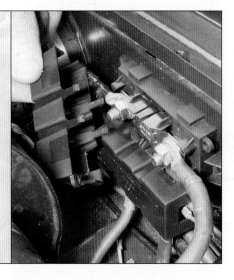

12 Run an earth cable, of the same size as the positive feed, from the negative terminal of the battery to the rear of the vehicle. Route both cables away from hot or moving parts and secure with cable ties.

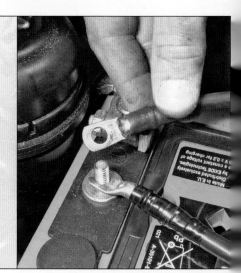

13 Fabricate a plate on which you can permanently mount the fixed half of the Anderson plug. Again, affix the cable to the plug using the heavy-duty solder connections.

14 Job done. It is merely a case of removing the protective plastic cap, which must be refitted after use . . .

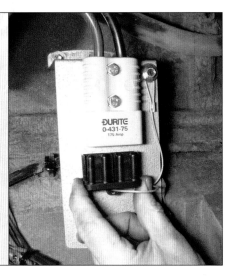

15 . . . and making the connection.

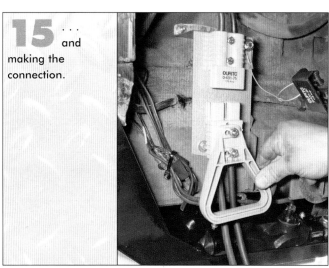

16 The portable winch works in the same way as the one we fitted to the front bumper, via a hand-held remote rocker switch and wander lead that plugs into the solenoid pack mounted on top of the winch itself. When required for use, the assembly hooks onto the tow ball and slots into the Anderson plug for its power supply. A neat solution to a piece of kit that is cumbersome if fitted permanently to the rear of the vehicle.

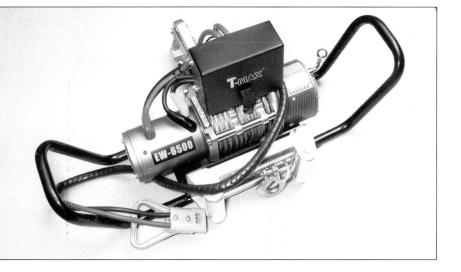

Front bumper

When fitting an aftermarket front bumper you will find that there are several different manufacturers making an all-steel construction unit. All are usually fitted with recovery and jacking points (to fit a hi-lift jack adapter), but your consideration has to be whether you should fit a winch bumper or non-winch version. A non-winch version will generally offer a better approach angle but other than that there is no difference.

On our project vehicle we opted for a front winch bumper from Bearmach. It is an all-steel construction, shaped to fit the vehicle and in a black powder coat finish. It sports two recovery points to attach shackles and a hi-lift jacking point on either side. The winch tray is integral to the unit and fitting is very straightforward. The main advantage of fitting this bumper is that, compared to the original Land Rover one, there are no plastic end caps fitted so it offers increased protection to the corners of the vehicle, whilst maintaining an aesthetically pleasing look.

Note: *Make sure that your bumper choice is compatible with your Discovery if it is fitted with airbags – consult your local dealer for more advice on this matter.*

1 The first task here is to remove the original bumper. A couple days prior to removal it is a good idea to spray all fixings with a penetrating oil to ease removal. To improve access apply the  handbrake, jack up the front of the vehicle and support on axle stands.

2 Slacken and remove all of the nuts and bolts that secure the bumper in position.

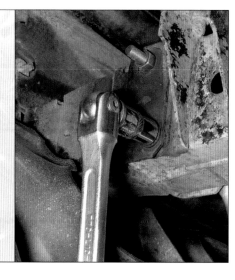

3 Recover the towing eye before lifting the bumper away from the vehicle.

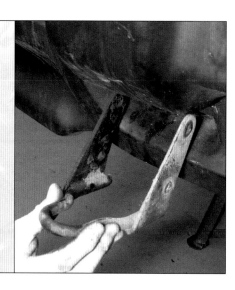

4 The front bumper we are fitting comes complete with built-in winch cradle and pre-drilled mounting holes for front headlamp washer jets and roo bar. Be aware that the bumper is heavy and will require at least two people to lift it onto the existing chassis mounting brackets.

5 The bumper is secured in place on these brackets using four nuts and bolts. Bumper installation completed, this is the time you would go fit a winch, roo bar and light grilles.

If self-recovery is important to you, then purchasing a front-mounted winch may be an option, whether it is hydraulic or electric powered. A winch can be very useful, especially if you intend exploring areas on your own. However, with a permanently fixed front winch you may find that, if you become stuck, your only option of self-recovery is forwards which may not be possible and, in fact, could lead you further into trouble. Sometimes the best or only way to get out is to go back the way you came, in which case a permanently fixed front winch is of no use.

We have chosen to fit a winch in the tray of our front bumper. The T-Max winch, supplied by Bearmach, is a very comprehensive kit and very straightforward to fit, albeit a bit of a heavy unit. It is powered by a 12V motor which is activated using solenoids mounted in a control box above the drum. A hand control is plugged into the front to operate the system and the cable is long enough for it to be operated by the driver whilst still in the vehicle, if necessary.

Before attempting any winching it is a good idea to familiarise yourself with all the controls and book yourself in for a training day. Winches can be extremely dangerous if not treated with care and respect. A vehicle that is stuck can generate very high loads and if something were to go wrong it could prove fatal. When a winch cable snaps or its mounting breaks, the stored energy in the cable under tension is unleashed at once. A flailing cable can cause considerable damage to property and/or people, so stand well clear and never attempt to work near a cable under tension. Always use a winch blanket over tensioned cables as this will help dissipate the energy in the cable should it give way.

Note:
- *ALWAYS wear gloves when handling winch wire.*
- *If a tree is being used as an anchor, protect the tree from damage by using a winch blanket.*

Winch cable alternatives

A wire cable supplied with a winch from new is replaceable with a couple of alternatives specifically designed for the job. Winch rope is a lightweight solution to the heavy cable, it will float on water and if it breaks will simply fall to the ground reducing the risk of serious injury. However, it cannot withstand the same heat generated by the winch that a steel cable can. It will require regular cleaning to remove dirt and debris which if left will chafe the structure of the rope, eventually weakening it. If it does break, it can be spliced back together and re-used whereas a steel cable cannot.

Winch web is similar to rope, but is in the form of a webbing strap. Properties are similar to that of the winch rope but generally it is not rated as strong; it is much cheaper to purchase, though.

1 First job is to fit the cable guide to the front bumper. This is secured in place using two nuts and bolts.

2 Next the winch control box is secured to the main body of the winch.

3 On the back of the control box there is an assortment of wires. Three of these are colour-coded and are of a similar length – a red, black and yellow cable complete with colour coded protective sleeves ...

4 ... these cables must be bolted to the corresponding colour-coded terminals on the winch motor. Smear some petroleum jelly on these connections after they have been made, prior to covering with the protective boot.

5 The longer black cable, complete with ring terminal, is then connected to the underside of the winch motor.

6 The captive nuts must then be placed carefully into the mounting holes at the base of the winch.

7 The winch can then be lifted into the cradle on the front bumper.

8 From the underside of the bumper the winch assembly is bolted into place using four anti-theft bolts.

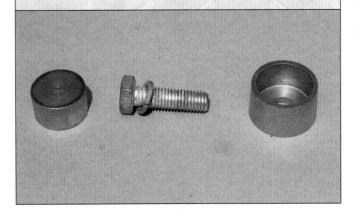

9 Fit the bolt housings and bolts into the mounting holes. Tighten the bolts.

10 Then, using a hammer, hit the anti-tamper cap up inside the housing. The only way to get these beauties off is to drill them out – too much effort for the opportunist thief, so should keep your expensive purchase safe.

11 Feed the end of the cable through the guide and secure the shackle in place on the cable.

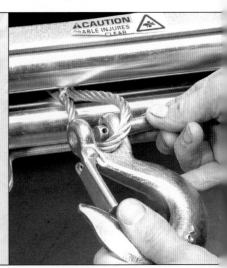

12 If not already done, disconnect the battery earth lead(s). Route the heavy red and black cables to the battery, securing them away from hot or moving parts. It is strongly recommended that the positive feed is via a fusible link as shown here. Check the winch manufacturer's specification to find out the maximum current draw. Also consider fitting an isolator switch as shown in the wiring diagram so that the power supply can be cut in case of emergency.

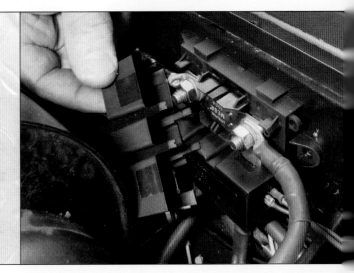

13 The black cable is then connected to the battery negative terminal.

14 The remote control to operate the winch is then simply plugged into the front of the control box.

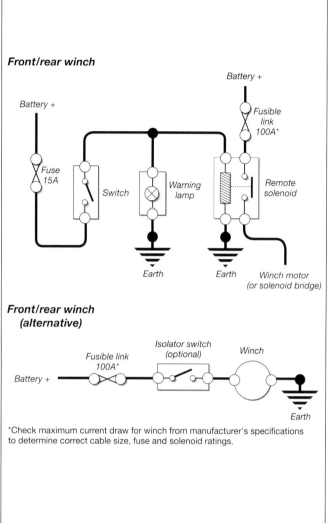

Front/rear winch

Battery +

Battery +

Fuse 15A

Switch

Warning lamp

Fusible link 100A*

Remote solenoid

Earth

Earth

Winch motor (or solenoid bridge)

Front/rear winch (alternative)

Battery +

Fusible link 100A*

Isolator switch (optional)

Winch

Earth

*Check maximum current draw for winch from manufacturer's specifications to determine correct cable size, fuse and solenoid ratings.

15 Remember to refit the waterproof cover on the front of the control box after use.

After installation and prior to its first use the cable should be stretched. To do this, unwind the complete length of cable. Attach a suitable load to the hook end such as another vehicle with the handbrake off, and preferably on a slight downhill slope away from the winch vehicle. Operate the winch to pull in the rolling load. When this is done the installation is complete.

Weathershields

Anyone who has driven a Discovery with the window open in even a little rain will have noticed a mini waterfall when cornering that seems to come in and run down the door card. This rain water spills off the end of the gutter rail and it can be prevented by fitting shields to the windows. Weathershields will deflect the water so that it runs off past the window instead of through it. They are also very useful when it is not raining and you like the window open for a little ventilation when on the move, as they deflect airflow around the window making driving your Discovery a little less like driving in a wind tunnel.

1 Lower the front window right down and, using a flat-bladed screwdriver, remove the guide that keeps the glass in the runner.

2 The shield can now be offered into place by slotting it into the window frame channel, lower end first . . .

3 . . . followed by the upper edge. It is necessary to gently flex the shield a little in order to achieve this, but do take considerable care or you may snap it in half.

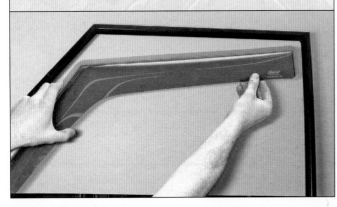

4 Ensure the shield sits perfectly within the window frame channel. Ask an assistant to hold the shield in place whilst you fully close then open the window five times. To ensure the shield sits in place permanently you may find it necessary to shave off a little of the plastic lip that wedges itself onto the window outer sealing strips.

When off-roading or on expedition in your Discovery, there is always the possibility of a rollover in difficult conditions, so a roll cage is very useful in protecting yourself and your passengers. When choosing a roll cage it is important to consider what level of protection you require. A basic rollover hoop behind the front seats will provide minimum protection in the event of a roll, whereas a full Camel Trophy style cage will offer complete protection but at a higher price.

Whatever cage you choose, make sure that it is fixed to the chassis and not just bolted to the floorpan, as this may buckle in the event of a rollover. Some designs of cages are purely cosmetic and don't offer a great deal of protection. One that is manufactured to competition specifications will offer the best level of protection.

Nudge/roo bar

There are several types of nudge bar available to buy nowadays:

- A full bar with integral lamp grilles designed to be fitted to a standard Discovery although slight trimming of the valance may be required.
- An A-bar which is essentially the same as a nudge bar, but without the extended pieces to cover the headlamp/indicator areas.
- A nudge bar that is designed to fit to the flat horizontal surface of a winch bumper. It is this type that we will be showing how to fit on our Discovery.

Most bars of any design will incorporate brackets for attaching auxiliary lighting, which is better than drilling through the front bumper to mount lights which one day you may wish to remove, eliminating any unsightly holes in the bumper that would also be a point of weakness for corrosion.

Once fitted, the bars will offer increased protection to the front of your vehicle from wayward branches or other such obstacles. Bush wires can also be attached to these bars to offer protection to the windscreen and sides of your vehicle (see *Bush wires*). Fitting of all types of bars is simple enough, but be careful as some styles may obscure your number plate.

Note: *Make sure that your choice of nudge bar is compatible with your Discovery if airbags are fitted. Fitting a nudge bar may change the crush characteristics of your vehicle – if in doubt speak to your local Land Rover dealer. As always, ensure you tell your insurance company about any modifications that take place to your vehicle as fitting such kit may result in a difference in the premium you pay. And be aware that there are proposals to make the fitting of nudge bars etc illegal. (At the time of writing it's not clear whether this will apply to all vehicles, or just to new models going forward.)*

The nudge bar we are fitting, supplied by the helpful folks at Bearmach, matches up perfectly with the pre-drilled front bumper mounting holes which makes fitting easy and relatively fuss free.

1 We are showing the process of mounting a nudge bar to an aftermarket bumper, not the original Land Rover one. The nudge bar weighs quite a lot and so requires a fairly beefy bumper to take the strain of it.

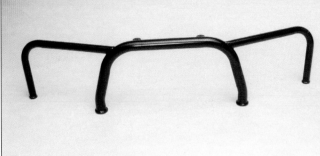

2 You can fit this bar one of two ways – either bolt the bar to the bumper on the floor and then lift the whole assembly into position on the vehicle and secure with the necessary fixings . . .

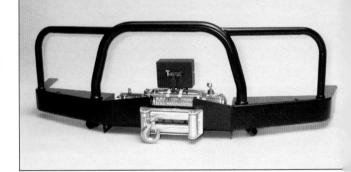

3 . . . or with the bumper already in place on the vehicle, simply lift the bar into place, aligning it with the holes in the front bumper. Bolt the bar into place using four bolts and washers – two of which are located at the

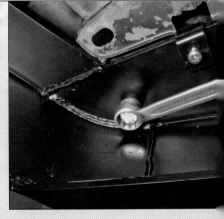

either end of the bar and 2 in the centre section. Tighten the bolts fully and the task is completed.

If your vehicle, like ours, is so high due to larger tyres and a suspension lift, that climbing onto the rear bumper to access the rear ladder and roof rack is becoming difficult, or you regularly transport passengers in the 'dickie' seats in the boot, you may consider fitting a rear step. Our step utilises the rear tow ball mounting bolts for its fixings, so fitment is very straightforward, but note: if you are using your vehicle off-road, please be aware that this kit is easily damaged due to its design. Departure angles are also hindered by the rear step, so consider using it as an occasional accessory, removing it from the vehicle when not required.

1 The rear step will be attached to the rear tow bracket, bolted in place by the tow ball.

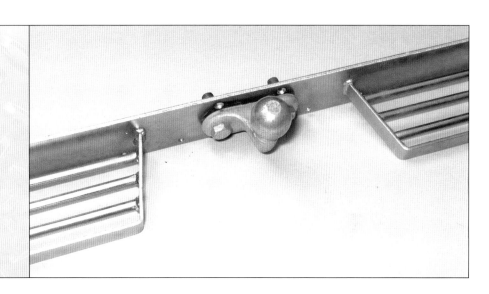

2 Apply some threadlocking compound to the bolts of the tow ball.

3 Finally, simply bolt the tow ball onto the bracket, tighten the retaining nuts fully and the task is complete.

Roof rack

For expedition use you may find that a roof rack would be useful, especially for carrying items such as waffle boards/sand ladders, jerry cans or maybe a roof tent.

There are quite a few manufacturers who can supply different types of roof rack, but they must be well-built and securely fitted to the vehicle, otherwise they may crack or break up when off-road. Weight for weight, roof racks of tubular design are stronger than box section designs, and they should be powder coated or galvanised to prevent corrosion.

Full-length expedition roof racks are a useful accessory but it should be noted that the rack on its own may be close to the limit for the roof weight specified by Land Rover. The better-designed racks will have their support legs positioned in-line with the main roof pillars of your vehicle, ie, the legs should be fixed to the vehicle at the top of the A, B, C and D pillars rather than in between these points, as the load is better distributed and supported.

The roof rack can be fitted with a floor if need be, as we have done. We used marine grade plywood painted in a waterproof stain. This is an ideal base if you wish to sleep on the roof to avoid snakes and other creatures whilst on expedition. An access ladder can also be fitted to make climbing up to the rack easier (see *Rear Ladder* section).

Another advantage of creating a wooden platform is that if you intend to visit hot countries, it will go some way towards helping to keep the interior temperatures of the vehicle down) in a similar way to a safari roof.

Some manufacturers include brackets on their racks to mount auxiliary front and rear lighting to, as this avoids drilling the vehicle body and causing water leaks if not adequately sealed.

On our project vehicle we have chosen to fit a genuine Land Rover roof rack. It uses gutter mounted fixings and raised sides to help retain the load.

1 Bolting the roof rack together is very straightforward, as most kits come with detailed assembly instructions.

2 Once the rack has been constructed you need to think about covering the base with a suitable material such as marine plywood to prevent items falling through the bars. We used a thread insert gun (rivnut gun with corresponding rivnuts) so that we could bolt the plywood to the rack securely. Threadlock applied to the threads of the bolts is a good idea.

3 It is imperative that you apply an all-weatherproof, waterproof stain to the plywood to stop the wood from rotting. This needs to be re-applied at least once a year. Depending on what you want to fit to the roof rack, you may need to fabricate a series of brackets. Our workshop mechanic constructed his own set of heavy-duty brackets to secure the waffle boards, ground anchor kit and hi-lift jack to the floor. It is possible to source ready-made mounting brackets for such items as the jerry can as additional purchases – enquire when you buy the kit. **Note:** *When lifting the rack on the roof of your Discovery, it is preferable to have someone strong at each corner of the rack lifting, as it is VERY heavy, particularly with the brackets on it. We suggest that you lift the rack into position then fix the brackets afterwards.*

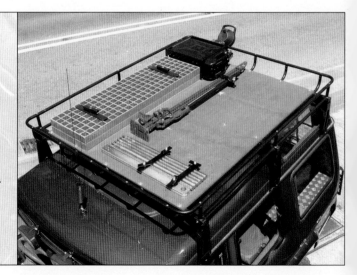

If you are modifying your Discovery and fitting extra large tyres you will find it is necessary to trim away some of the surrounding body panels to accommodate the extra rubber. To finish off the look of the panels after the trimming has been carried out, wheel arch extensions are a great way of creating a nice finish as well as helping stay within the confines of the law, and cover the extra width of the new tyres that would otherwise protrude from the side of the vehicle if uncovered.

The arches we have fitted to our Discovery supplied by Scorpion Racing are of fibreglass moulding, which can be secured to the existing panels by rivets or screws. The kit is available in both 5- and 3-door versions, and particularly straightforward to fit to the latter. A 5-door kit is slightly more complicated to fit as it involves cutting the rear doors. If unsure, ask your local body repairer for advice or contact the supplier of the kit.

1 Place some masking tape along the bottom flat surface of the swage line above the wheel arch. Offer the arch extension into place on the vehicle and mark the centre point of the arch.

2 Have an assistant hold the extension perfectly still in place whilst you mark the areas on the side protection moulding/rubbing strip that needs to be cut away. Obviously you only want to cut away the excess trim so that the side trim butts up against the arch and no gap can be seen once the arch has been fitted.

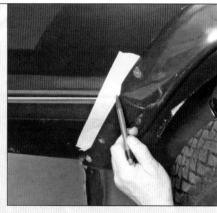

3 Remove the extension from the vehicle and cut away the unwanted trim. When the section has been cut, use a flat-bladed screwdriver to lever the trim away. It is held in place by strong double-sided tape.

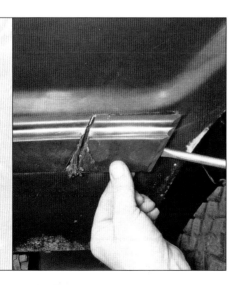

4 You may notice on one side that the actual profile of the extension needs to be modified in order to fit the shape of the side trim. So mark the area on the arch . . .

5 . . . and trim the fibreglass accordingly.

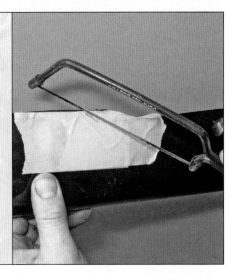

6 On the front, prior to cutting, the wheel arch liners must be removed. Note that refitment of the liner after cutting may not be possible. Now it comes to the part where the arches on the vehicle need to be cut off; remember you will need some metal body left to fix the extension to. Using a suitable cutting tool, cut away the existing curved profile of the arch.

7 On a clean flat surface, drill through the mounting holes on the extension.

8 Fit the extension in the correct position on the car and ask an assistant to hold it securely whilst you fit the protective waterproof beading all the way round the extension.

9 With the assistant holding the extension securely in place, drill the holes for the self-tapping screws in the body of the vehicle.

10 Once all the holes have been drilled, screw or rivet the arch in place permanently and then trim away any excess protective beading.

11 Use a large bead of silicone sealant at each end of the arch extension to bond it to the car fully. Two clamps will hold the extension in place until the sealant dries.

12 The rock sliders fitted to our vehicle needed to be removed and cut to fit the new shorter side sills of the vehicle. Depending on what tools you have to hand this may prove not to be a DIY job. **Note:** *The sill plastic protective covers will also need to be trimmed when cutting the arches away if the standard trims are left in place.*

13 Cutting the rock sliders sounds easier than it actually is as they are made from incredibly thick, tough metal. You need to use a pretty impressive cutting tool to get the job done.

14 With the excess removed you will need to weld a plate over the open ends of the rock sliders. If this is not possible to do at home, ask a local fabricator to do the job for you instead. Once cut and welded, refit the sliders to the vehicle.

15 The final task that may be applicable to you is to cut the chequer plate body panels to fit the shorter sides of the vehicle.

Custom panels

When installing a multitude of extras to your Discovery as we have done, we found it useful to design and fabricate dedicated mounting panels to fit auxiliary switches in, and more importantly to avoid drilling lots of unsightly holes in the dashboard when mounting equipment.

The first panel we made was designed to sit on top of the existing dashboard, which meant we could bolt equipment to it and run the associated wiring underneath it so it wouldn't be on view. To make this panel we made a template of the area and sent that to a fabricator to make out of a sheet of aluminium. The plate would need to be removable to facilitate mounting equipment to in the future. The complete dashboard assembly was removed to have fixings placed from the underside of it, onto which the top plate would screw, therefore providing us with a removable mounting plate.

The second panel was created to house the many switches we would need to fit to power and control electrical ancillaries such as work lights (front and rear), air locking diff and compressor, and isolation switch for the electric fan. The major benefits of an overhead panel such as this is that all the switch gear is kept together and immediately to hand to the operator. A template of the overhead storage area was made and given to our fabricators for manufacture out of sheet aluminium. Holes were punched out for the switches and then it was folded to shape. When fitted into the vehicle a utility blade was run around the headlining where the edges of the panel would fit so that, when screwed into place, it would 'seat' into the headlining for a neater finish. The original storage area was removed entirely and the captive nuts in the roof used as securing points for our switch panel, albeit using longer screws, ensuring the screws did not pierce the roof skin when fitted.

Side body panels

1 Before fitting anything, take a moment to unpack the kit to check you have all the relevant pieces. Then determine which panel goes where, whilst checking that each panel fits the area properly.

2 Starting at the front of the vehicle mask up the top and bottom edges of the area. This will enable you to mark the areas for drilling and provide a non-slip surface for the drill. The holes in the panels are pre-drilled which makes life a little easier.

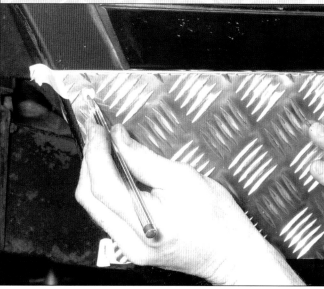

3 Drill the correct-sized holes for the pop-rivets you are using.

4 Then as you may have already guessed, all you have left to do is rivet the panel in place. Continue the above process until all panels are secured on both sides of the vehicle.

Note: *It was necessary for us to remove these panels at a later date in order to fit a wheel arch kit to accommodate our huge 33" wheels. If you plan to fit an arch extension kit you may find it easier to fit that first, as the chequer plate panels are only supplied to contour a standard wheel arch radius and will need modifying.*

Tailgate

1 Undo the two retaining 10 mm bolts and remove the large handle from inside the tailgate.

2 Lift the interior tailgate lock handle and undo the retaining screw, then remove the surrounding handle trim from the door card.

3 On our model there were no rear speaker assemblies – consult your Workshop Manual if your vehicle has, as removal of the speakers is necessary. By levering gently with a suitable tool, release the trim panel studs that are located around the outside edge of the panel. Once all studs are released the trim panel can be lifted way from the vehicle.

4 Apply masking tape to the outside edge of the tailgate door and mark the areas where it is not safe to drill. We shall be using self-tapping screws to secure the chequer plate panel in place so it is imperative to protect certain areas of the door whilst ensuring the panel is firmly held in place.

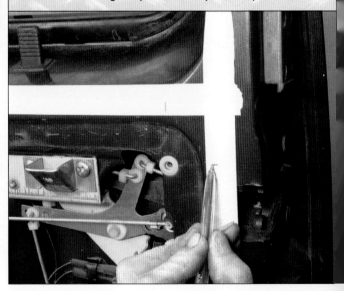

5 Now apply masking tape to the outside edges of the chequer panel and offer the panel into position. It is now possible to mark on the panel where it is safe to drill the holes for the screws.

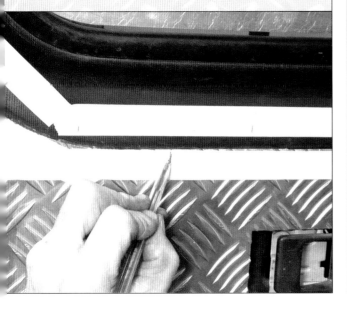

6 Drill the marked holes using a suitable-sized bit. Deburr any rough edges that may result from drilling the holes.

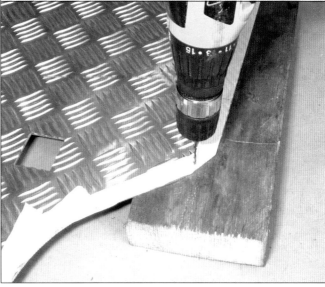

7 Ask an assistant to hold the panel in place on the door whilst you drill the holes in the tailgate door. After securing the panel in a couple of strategic positions you can complete the procedure without aid.

8 All that's left to do now is refit the lock handle trim and handle. After a couple of checks to see that the door opens and closes without fouling you can stand back and admire your work!

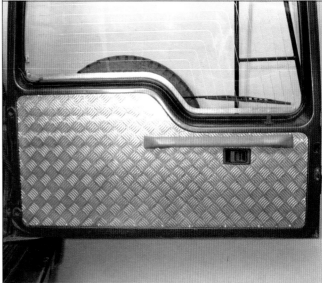

When modifying a Discovery for off-road or expedition use, protection of the vehicle is always an important topic to consider, and here we are looking at the bonnet area. A chequer plate panel, usually made of aluminium for weight-saving purposes, can be made or purchased and is affixed to the top side of the existing bonnet. This extra 'skin' will enable you to place more weight on the bonnet without causing damage to the relatively thin original skin. By 'weight' we mean that you are able to carry some recovery/camping equipment on the bonnet if need be, secured under a luggage net. Also, if you happen to find yourself stuck in a deep water section for example, it is possible to walk or crawl across the bonnet to attach a recovery rope to the front end (if you forgot to do this before entering the water!).

Another point to consider is if the vehicle has been fitted with roof-mounted spot lights, it is a good idea to paint the chequer plate matt black before fitting it. This will reduce any reflections in the previously shiny surface of the plate when the lamps are on. Alternatively, if you have roof-mounted lamps but do not require the extra protection plate it is possible to create a matt black area on the bonnet by either simply painting it, or applying a vinyl covering which when not required can be removed.

1 Offer the plate into position on the bonnet with the aid of an assistant, and check for any fitment issues. If you have fitted a bonnet pod, the plate will need to be marked and trimmed to accommodate the pod, so do this now.

2 Still with the plate in place, mark and drill a series of holes around the edge of the chequer plate in order to fix it securely to the bonnet.

3 To eliminate any glare in the windscreen from the shiny aluminium, the chequer plate will need to be painted black. On a surface such as this you will need to use the correct primer and paint. We are using a special etch primer that will suit the uneven profile of the surface of the plate. A second coat may be required. **Note:** *Always paint in a well-ventilated area and use several lighter layers rather than one thick layer of paint, which is likely to cause runs, which aren't aesthetically pleasing.*

4 Once the surface is completely dry, the corresponding black paint can be applied. A second coat will almost certainly be required. Check the instructions on the can for drying times.

5 Lift the plate into position once again with the help of assistant and position centrally on the bonnet. Bolt or screw down the plate depending on what style of fixings you've chosen to use –

we used pan-head Allen key type screws and Nyloc nuts just for a more pleasing look.

When using your Discovery for regular off-road use or for expeditions you will find that you need to carry a lot of kit with you. All kit needs to be mounted securely in the vehicle and ideally be easily accessible without the need to unload everything to find the item you are looking for. Primarily, gear also needs to be stored securely: a hi-lift jack thrown in the boot is fine, until you encounter rough terrain, ascents/descents or side slopes. The last thing you want is to be hit round the head by a jack that wasn't properly secured. Insecure loads may shift and, on a perilous side slope this is not a good time for your load to decide to change sides in the boot. It is imperative that your load-carrying area is separated by a strong guard, or that the items kept in the boot are secured so they cannot move about.

Secondly, particularly if you use your Discovery for overland trips, it is important that luggage is organised into some sort of priority. When designing your own load space it is a good idea to create several 'hidden' cubby holes that can be used for storing high value items, such as cameras, binoculars, passports, etc. You may also find it useful to add some power points (12V and 230V) and some additional lighting, depending on the use of the vehicle.

There are several suppliers of good quality storage solutions such as lightweight aluminium locking drawer systems, shelving, window grilles, and so on, although it is possible to design your own storage system using plywood for example (see above). This system uses a combination of drawers and shelves with storage boxes secured in place, which can be removed if desired.

Luggage or map pockets are another useful, inexpensive piece of kit that will secure smaller, lighter items and can be positioned virtually anywhere within the vehicle.

In our project Discovery we have opted to create an alloy chequer load space. This has the advantage of being strong and durable, easily cleaned and the area remains wholly useable as before. Tie-down points can be bolted to the sheet metal and ratchet straps used to secure any loads to these points. 12 volt power and lighting was fitted at the same time to create an extremely useful area within the vehicle for an off-road enthusiast to develop further to meet their personal needs.

Hopefully these pictures will give you some ideas on what to do in your own load area, whether you do the work yourself or purchase pre-fabricated units.

Rear interior load light (fluorescent tube type)

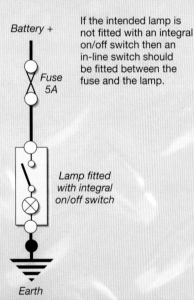

Battery +

Fuse 5A

If the intended lamp is not fitted with an integral on/off switch then an in-line switch should be fitted between the fuse and the lamp.

Lamp fitted with integral on/off switch

Earth

1 First job is to remove the trim panels from the load area so that it is possible to use them as templates.

2 The trim is held in place with a series of body clips and an assortment of screws that have been fixed to the panels over the years as the original fixings broke or were lost.

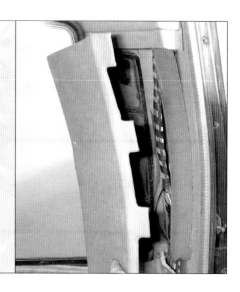

3 Remove the seat belts from their rear anchor points on the floor of the load area. Undo the sill trim and remove the carpet.

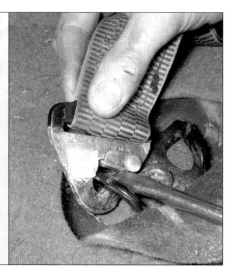

4 Remove the seat belts from their anchor points on the wheel arches on either side, then remove the carpet from the arches.

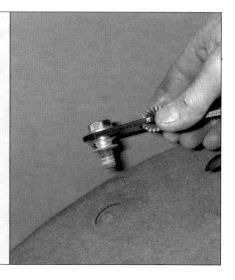

5 Finally remove the thick rubber matting and the load area should now be bare.

6 We recommend you get any extensive corrosion or holes fixed now, particularly if there is any occurring around the seat belt mounts, as this area is a bit of a water trap. A

replacement boot floor panel can be purchased and fitment is fairly straightforward.

7 Along the bottom edges of the windows it will be necessary to fit battens of wood to screw the chequer plate panels onto . . .

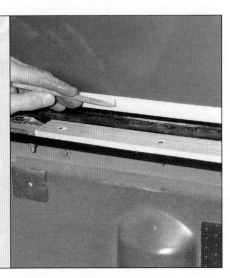

8 . . . as well as fitting wood battens to the floor of the vehicle so that the panels can be secured at the base, too.

9 Using cardboard, create templates of the area, bearing in mind you will need access to the rear of the light clusters so leave enough space in the new panel for this.

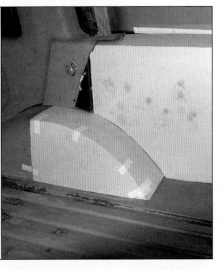

10 When you are finished you should have something that looks like this.

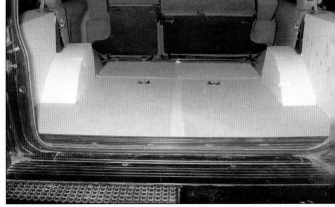

11 Why not completely finish the look by creating a template for the backs of the seats? Then when the door is open all you will see is the chequer plate.

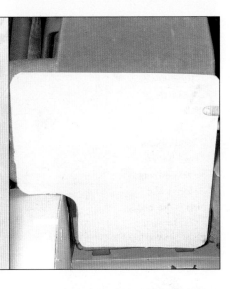

12 Purely due to time constraints we sent our templates off to a local specialist who laser cut our panels to size and welded our wheel arch chequer plates together. It

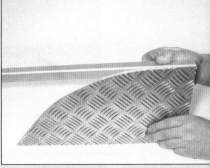

is possible to do this job yourself even on the hardest parts such as the wheel arch areas. Firstly cut out the two sections of chequer plate from your cardboard templates and then find some angled alloy.

13 Cut slots into the alloy angle so that you are able to bend it to shape the curved edge of the chequer plate.

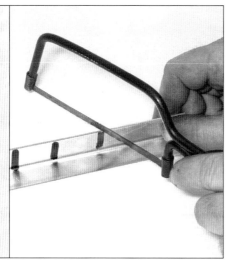

14 Drill a hole through either end of the chequer plate and the angle, then pop rivet the two pieces together.

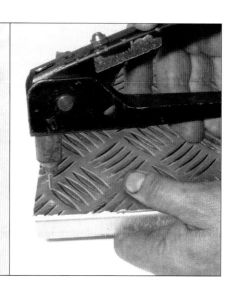

15 Cut away the excess length of angle.

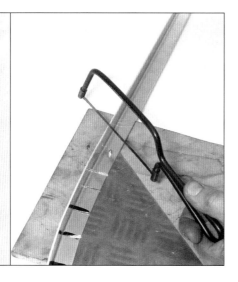

16 Take the top section of chequer plate and drill a mounting hole through that and the angle as before, then pop rivet the chequer plate to the angle.

17 Bend the top section of chequer plate to fit the profile of the other piece and drill a hole and pop rivet the plate to the angle.

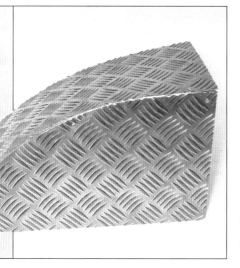

18 Use the rest of your templates to cut the chequer plate panels out and then screw them down inside the load area – you will be left with something that looks like this, which is the basis for you to start kitting out the load area as you desire.

Bush wires

Bush wires, or limb risers as they are sometimes known, are an important accessory to fit if you are venturing off-road in heavily vegetated areas. On expedition they also act as a very useful clothes line! When fitted to the vehicle correctly they contact and lift tree branches/bushes up to roof height as you pass, thus offering some degree of protection to the windscreen and side windows of the vehicle. They are best fitted to the leading edge of a roof rack and extend down to the top corners of the roo bar.

In the sequence below we have shown you how to fit them if you have neither a nudge bar or roof rack fitted. Only the location of the mounting brackets differs, the rest of the process is the same wherever you choose to mount the brackets. It is not really advisable to fit them to the thin alloy panels of your Discovery, as any large branches might pull the bracket bolts through the wing; a way to reinforce a wing-mounted bracket is to supplement it with another plate on the inside of the panel.

If you're wondering where to get wires and fittings like this, of course the usual off-road specialists will be able to help. Other sources include yacht chandlers - the wires are called stainless steel shrouds in yacht-speak - or a hardware shop.

Note: *Bush wires must only be used off-road because of the hazard they represent to pedestrians in the event of an accident.*

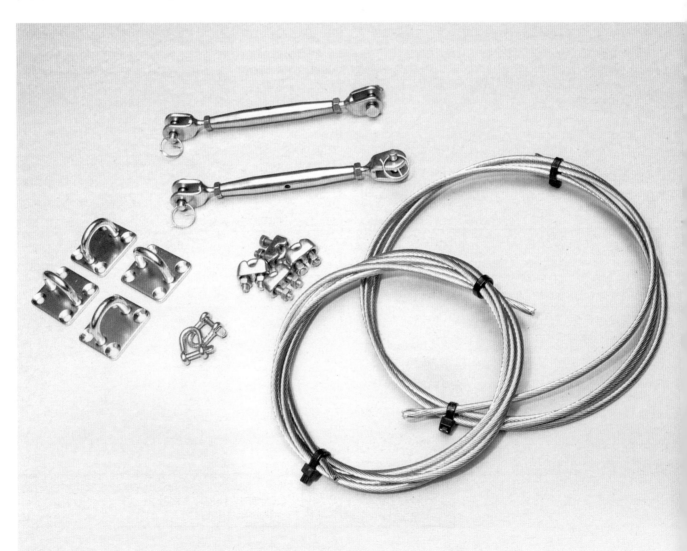

1 Select one of the mounting plates, offer into position on the front wing/roo bar and mark the holes for drilling. When deciding where to fit the plates, remember that you have to be able to open the bonnet with the wires fitted!

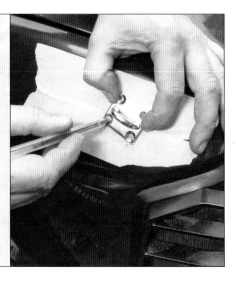

2 Using a second mounting plate repeat the above step, but position it on the roof/roof rack of the vehicle, ensuring that it is in line with the lower plate.

3 A clevis pin and spring clip are used to fix the tensioner to the lower mounting plate. Wind the tensioner ends most of the way out of the body so that the tensioner is at its longest.

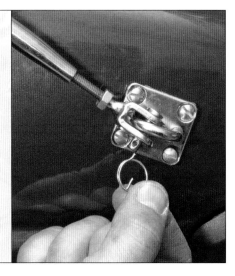

4 Take the cable and hook that through the end of the tensioner. The cable is then held in place using one of the four cable clamps. Repeat this step for the other end of the cable, however, this time ensure that the smaller shackle is fitted to the upper mounting plate, then hook the cable through that.

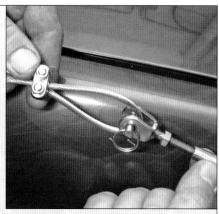

5 Adjust the cable length by repositioning the clamps if necessary, then turn the tensioner body to tighten the cable. Use an Allen key or similar through the hole in the tensioner body if necessary; secure by tightening the tensioner locknuts (arrowed). When satisfied, cut off any excess cable. Recheck the tension of the wires regularly when in use.

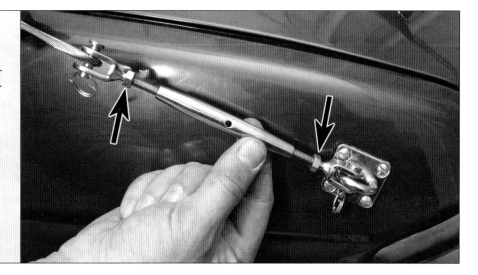

Rear ladder

If you have already fitted a roof rack to your Discovery then in order to access it properly it is a good idea to fit a rear door-mounted ladder. These can be purchased from many Land Rover specialists and are all generally fitted in the same way. Make sure, however, that the rear wiper operates correctly without fouling and that the rear number plate has not become obscured. The ladders are designed to be used with the door shut only, any attempts of using the ladder with the door even only slightly ajar may result in damage to the hinges or deformation of the door itself – you have been warned!

1 Offer the ladder into position on the left-hand side of the door.

2 Drill two holes in the top of the door large enough to fit the captive nuts supplied in the kit.

3 Insert the captive nuts into the mounting holes, then fit the bolts and washers and tighten fully. If you have access to one, use a rivnut tool to fit the captive nuts.

4 Holding the ladder in place, drill two pilot holes through each of the two lower mounting brackets.

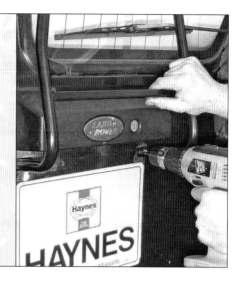

5 Drill four holes large enough to accommodate the captive nuts and insert them into the holes.

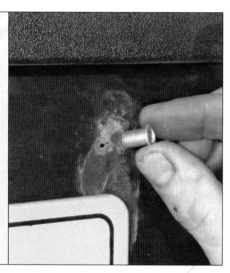

6 Place the metal template supplied in the kit, over the hole and insert the bolt complete with locknut, fully into the captive nut.

7 Counter-holding the bolt head, tighten the locknut fully against the metal plate, then loosen off the locknut and remove the nut, bolt and plate. This is the process of installing the captive nut in order for it to expand sufficiently and not be simply pulled out when the bolt is fitted into it. Repeat the process for the remaining three holes. Again, the rivnut tool is very useful here.

8 Refit the ladder to the vehicle and fit all the bolts and washers into the captive nuts, this time without the locknuts, and tighten fully. Installation is now completed.

Tinting windows

It's worth picking your day, and your working area, pretty carefully – on a windy day, there'll be more dust in the air, and it'll be a nightmare trying to stop the film flapping and folding onto itself while you're working.

Applying window tint is best done on a warm day (or in a warm garage), because the adhesive will begin to dry sooner. For fairly obvious reasons, don't try tinting when it's starting to get dark! It's a good idea to have a friend to help out with this job.

1 Make sure the window being tinted is clean – really clean – inside and out. Don't use glass cleaners (or any other product) containing ammonia or vinegar, since both will react with the film or its adhesive, and muck it up. Also clean the area around the window – it's too easy for stray dirt to attach itself to the film – and by the time you've noticed it, it could be too late. On door windows, wind them down slightly, to clean all of the top edge, then close them tight to fit the film.

2 Before you even unroll the film, take note – handle it carefully. If you crease it, you won't get the creases out – ever. First work out which way up the film is, by applying a small bit of sticky tape to the front and back side – use the tape to pull the films apart, just at one corner.

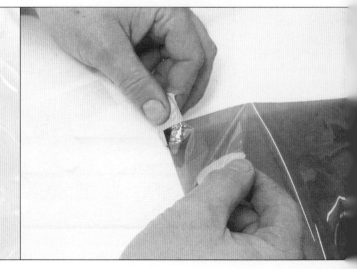

3 Lay the film onto the glass, with the clear side facing you. Unroll the film, and cut it roughly to the size of the window (on a door window, leave plenty at the bottom edge for now). Some kits have a logo on the film, which seems daft – tinting's difficult enough, without having to get a logo straight! The only benefit of a logo is to establish which layer is the tint. Make life easier – lose the logo.

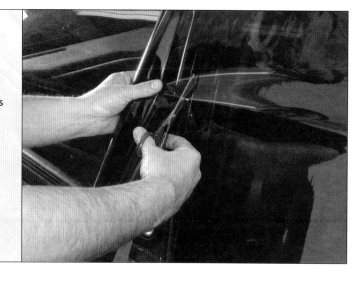

4 Spray the outside of the window with a weak soapy water solution. Try using one of those plant sprayers you can buy cheap in any DIY store, if your kit doesn't contain a sprayer.

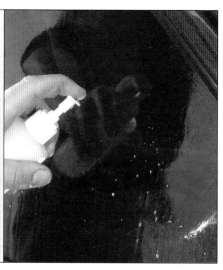

5 Lay the roughly-cut sheet of tint back onto the glass, and spray the outside of the film with soapy water . . .

6 . . . then use a squeegee to get out the air bubbles, sticking the film to the outside of the glass.

7 On a door window, trim the bottom edge to leave some excess to tuck down inside the door – this stops the film peeling off on the bottom rubber when you roll the window down!

8 Using a sharp knife (and taking care not to damage your paint or the window rubber), trim round the outside of the window. An unimportant piece of plastic, similar to a credit card, is brilliant for tucking the film into the edges to get the shape right, but don't trim the film right to the absolute edge – leave a small, even, gap of just a few millimetres all round (this helps to get rid of excess water when you squeegee it on the inside – you'll see).

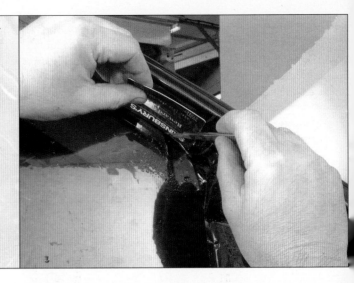

9 Now go inside, and prepare for receiving the tint. On fixed glass, waterproof the side trim panels in anticipation of the soapy water which will be used, by taping on some plastic sheet. Spray the inside of the glass with the soapy solution.

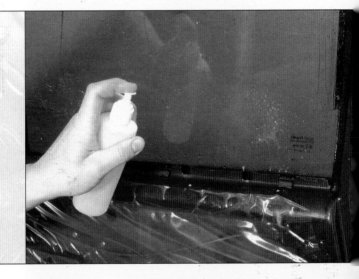

10 Back outside, it's time to separate the films. Use two pieces of sticky tape to pull the films slightly apart at one corner. As the films come apart, spray more solution onto the tinted piece underneath, to help it separate cleanly. Try not to lift the tint film too much off the glass when separating, as this increases the risk of creasing.

11 Have your willing helper on standby, to assist with transferring the film to the inside (a prime time for messing it all up). Peel the tint film off the glass, keeping it as flat as you can. Without letting it fold onto itself, move it inside the vehicle and place it fairly accurately on the inside of the glass. The surface which was outside should now be on the inside of the glass (now that you've cut it, it will only fit one way!). Carefully slide the film into the corners, keeping it flat.

12 On a door window, use your unimportant plastic to tuck the film into the door – try to stick it to the glass by wedging-in a wad of paper cloth too.

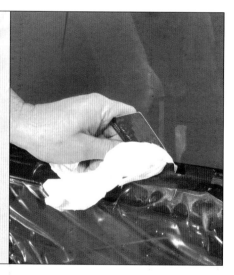

13 Spray the film with the soapy water . . .

14 . . . then carefully start to squeegee it into place, working from top to bottom. We found that, to get into the corners, it was easier to unscrew the blade from the squeegee, and use that on its own for some of it.

15 You'll end up with a few strips at the bottom, which seemingly will not stick to the glass. Don't panic. First, soak up any excess water at the base of the film, with paper towels. Now using a hot-air gun to very gently warm the film should help to finish drying, and encourage the film to stick. Be careful squeegee-ing the film when it's dry – risk of damage. Don't lift the film off the glass – the adhesive will stick, given time. Persistence pays off.

ELECTRICAL

Split charge system

230V inverter with 3-pin socket

12V sockets in load area

Auxiliary fusebox

Nudge bar mounted lights

Bonnet pod lights

Headlight protection grilles

Rear light cluster protection grilles

Roof-mounted front lights

Roof-mounted rear working light

CB radio and antenna

Distance/trip meter

Satellite navigation

Split charge system

Depending on what you use your Discovery for, sooner or later you might want to add some auxiliary electrical equipment to it. Some circuits are fine to be wired to the vehicle's own wiring system but the larger current-consuming items are best run from a second battery – for example winches or auxiliary lighting, particularly if you use your Discovery for camping and you want to run a fridge with the engine switched off. To do this, a second deep-cycle battery is best fitted on the opposite side to the main battery and will be kept charged by fitting what is known as a split charge system.

There are many different types of split charge system on the market but we have chosen a National Lunar kit. Discussions with leading 4X4 specialists have produced this comprehensive system that has been specifically designed not to interfere with the vehicle's existing electrical systems. It comes in three parts – an intelligent solenoid, dual battery monitor and a fusible links. It makes sure that the main battery is charged first and fully then switches the charge to the auxiliary battery.

The extra battery(s) and clamp are additional purchases – it is worth replacing the main battery with a deep cycle one, too, if the budget allows it. When buying batteries it is preferable to buy ones that have been designed for the job – those that can cope with continual discharge and recharge cycles. The Exide Maxxima Deep cycle batteries we used have rapid recharging times due to lower internal resistance, offer two pairs of terminals for bolting auxiliary wiring and are maintenance free.

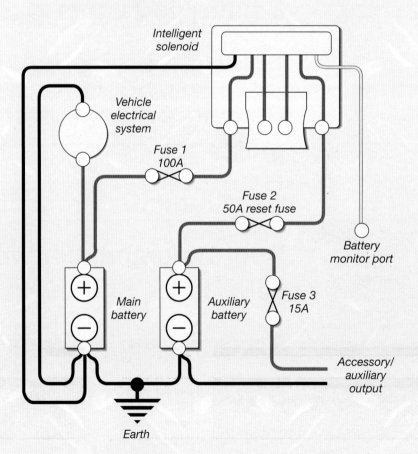

Split charging system

Intelligent solenoid

Vehicle electrical system

Fuse 1 100A

Fuse 2 50A reset fuse

Battery monitor port

Main battery

Auxiliary battery

Fuse 3 15A

Accessory/ auxiliary output

Earth

1 The first job will be to mount an auxiliary battery. As Discoveries were 'made for modifying' there is a perfect spot in the engine bay near the air cleaner that is just waiting to be filled with a battery. On your vehicle, such things as the air cleaner, PAS reservoir, etc, may need relocating first.

2 If you found the space that would be occupied by the battery was just a bit too big and even with a clamp on the battery would be prone to movement, simply cable tie a batten of wood to the body to help eliminate all movement by wedging the battery in place.

3 Battery retaining clamps are very inexpensive to buy and available from most car accessory outlets. The most trouble you will have with fitting this is perhaps the inconvenience of drilling some mounting holes. On our vehicle we didn't even have to do that.

4 Bolt an earth strap to vehicle metal in a position where it can comfortably be connected to the battery negative terminal. Put the battery in place to check that the strap fits, then disconnect it again while you install the split charge system.

5 Disconnect all battery earth leads. The first job is to mount the intelligent solenoid in an upright position in a suitable area in the engine bay. By suitable we mean an area that will prevent water ingress to the solenoid.

6 Next install the 100A fusible link as close as possible to the main battery and connect to battery positive.

Cable Sizes

The cables used in this installation must be adequate for the fuse ratings - 100A for the main battery and 50A for the slave. The same goes for the earth link cable between the batteries. (Do not be tempted to use the chassis for the earth return. It is important that the batteries be linked by their own earth cable.) It is better to err on the side of safety and fit heavier cable than needed in order to avoid problems due to voltage drop or cables overheating.

7 Connect the free terminal of the fusible link to the terminal marked Main Battery on the intelligent solenoid using a suitable red cable. **Note:** *Solder ring terminals to the wiring and use heat shrink to protect the connections. Use the correct type terminals for the cable size.*

8 Then connect another red wire from the terminal on the intelligent solenoid marked Auxiliary Battery to the 50A reset fuse that will be mounted close to the auxiliary battery. Connect another red wire from the fuse to the positive terminal of the auxiliary battery.

9 Connect a suitable black cable from the negative terminal of the main battery to the negative of the auxiliary battery.

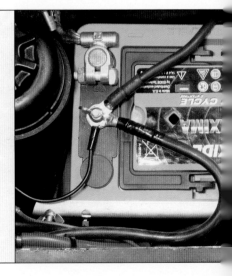

10 Connect the black wire from the intelligent solenoid to the negative of the main battery. The circuit is now powered and will result in the green light on the solenoid flashing once.

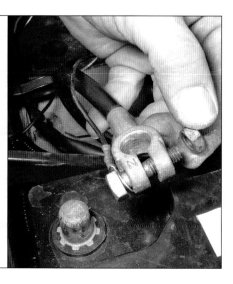

11 Plug the battery monitor cable into the port on the intelligent solenoid. The cable then needs to be routed through the bulkhead (remember to fit a grommet in the hole you are drilling) to the area on the dash where you are mounting the monitor.

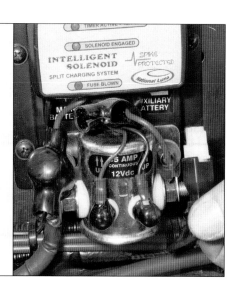

12 Inside the cabin construct a plate or bracket for the monitor – we've used magnetic pads to hold it in place so it is easy to remove the monitor for closer inspection.

13 Firmly push the remaining plug into the battery monitor and position the monitor on the bracket.

14 Refit all protective caps to the terminals of the intelligent solenoid. Then ensure that all wiring is safely cable tied out of the way or to the existing loom where possible. As with all electrical equipment it is important to sit down and read the operating instructions carefully. Supplied with this kit are pages of information on the different functions of the battery monitor alone. It would be a good idea to keep this information somewhere safe inside the vehicle until you are confident in reading the meters and understanding how the solenoid works.

230V inverter with 3-pin socket

Depending on the way you use your Discovery, you may find the need to have a mains 230V supply in your vehicle. Whether this is for running a laptop computer with navigational programs, such as memory map, or using light hand tools, an inverter is a way of transforming 12 volts dc into 230 volts ac.

There are quite a few different capacity inverters available from about 150 watts up to 2000 watts. However the greater the output, the more load you will put onto your vehicle's battery and this may not be ideal if you already have a large number of auxiliary electrical circuits in use.

Position is important, not only for accessing the 3-pin socket on the unit (although it is possible to relocate this if necessary) but also because the inverter contains a small cooling fan which operates when it is used, and requires a reasonable amount of airflow around it to keep it cool. You may find that at times it will overheat and temporarily shut down.

The inverter we have chosen to fit is manufactured by Ring and is rated at 500 watts, which is fine to run a portable TV, computer, phone charger or similar electrical items. For easy access and to make sure we have adequate cooling, we chose to mount the unit in the glovebox on the dash because we feel it would be of most use to someone powering a laptop to use with satellite navigation systems. This involved cutting a section away from the rear of the glovebox to allow for good airflow. Despite this, the fitting of the unit is very straightforward, as only two electrical connections need to be made.

1 The amount of work involved in mounting the inverter will differ depending on where in the vehicle you choose to locate it. Two retaining screws underneath at the back and three screws under the top edge release the glovebox. For more information on removing any of the panels in the vehicle refer to the workshop manual.

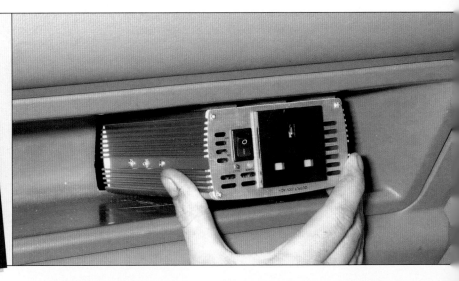

2 Mark the area that needs to be cut away to house the inverter. Again the amount of trimming may differ, depending on where you mount yours and whether you wish only the three-pin socket to be on show.

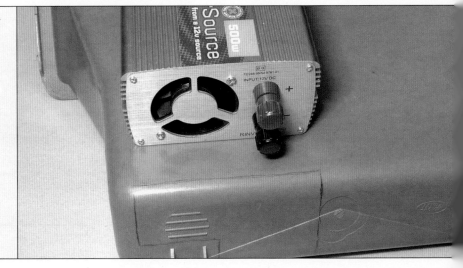

3 After trimming panels remove any rough edges with a file.

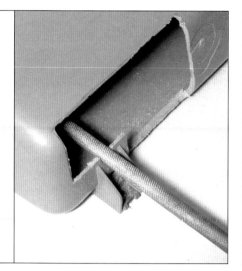

4 For ease of removal at any time some double-sided foam tape is our preferred mounting method. This may not be a secure enough method if you are fitting your inverter in a different area, in which case some stronger mounting brackets may be required.

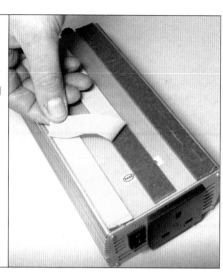

5 Wiring the inverter is simple as it only involves a fairly heavy-duty live and earth which connect to the relevant posts on the rear of the unit and then run straight down to the battery. If an auxiliary battery is fitted, it is preferable to connect the wires to that so the main battery is protected from being drained whilst appliances are run from the inverter with the engine off. Remember that a fusible link should be fitted in-line close to the battery.

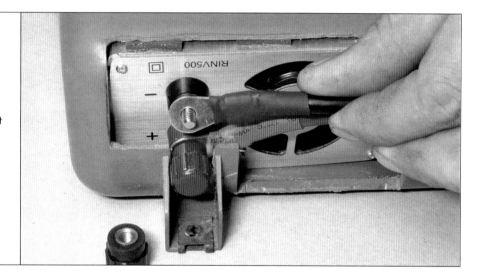

6 Finally with the wiring complete refit the glovebox, or any trim that you have removed to fit yours, and the installation is complete.

12V sockets in load area

When equipping your vehicle for off-road or expedition use, it is quite likely that at some stage you will need to power some portable 12V equipment such as a hand lamp, electric cool box, etc. It is a good idea to fit two or three accessory sockets somewhere on the vehicle rather than relying on crocodile clips on the battery for connections. If your vehicle is already fitted with an auxiliary battery, ideally these sockets should be powered from this battery so that you can run the appliances without having to run the engine, and avoid draining the main battery.

On our project vehicle we chose to fit two standard cigarette lighter style sockets in the rear load area for convenience. They are supplied without an element and with protective plastic caps that keep dirt out whilst not in use.

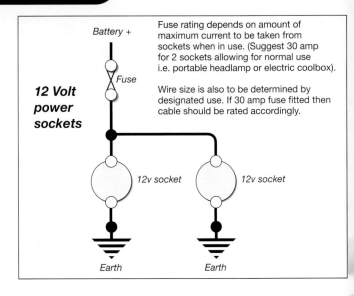

12 Volt power sockets

Fuse rating depends on amount of maximum current to be taken from sockets when in use. (Suggest 30 amp for 2 sockets allowing for normal use i.e. portable headlamp or electric coolbox).

Wire size is also to be determined by designated use. If 30 amp fuse fitted then cable should be rated accordingly.

1 First, decide where in the rear of the vehicle you will position the sockets – fairly near the rear door for practicality and in an easily-accessible location. When you have decided where, remove the trim panel and create two holes in it to house the sockets.

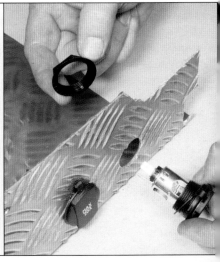

2 Insert the socket into the hole and tighten the plastic retaining nut.

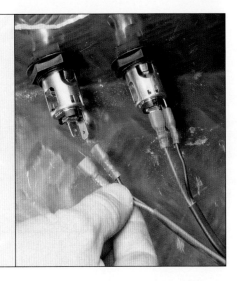

3 As you can see from the wiring diagram, the wiring up of the sockets is very straightforward. Connect the wires to the rear of the sockets. Check the sockets are working before you start refitting trim panels.

4 Refit the trim panel and the installation is complete.

When fitting any auxiliary electrical circuits to your Discovery, it is of paramount importance that each circuit is fused with the correctly-rated fuse. It is also an advantage to be able to access the fuse for a circuit quickly and easily if a replacement is needed. For this reason it is a good idea to fit one (or, like us, two) auxiliary fusebox. These can be purchased from most car accessory outlets or motor factors, and come in a variety of different styles and fitments. They normally come in 4, 6, or 8 way configurations, sometimes more.

It is a sensible idea to buy slightly bigger than you need, as any additional auxiliary circuits fitted in the future will already have a power supply sat there waiting for it.

In our Discovery we had a number of auxiliary electrical equipment systems and had little choice but to fit two eight-way fuseboxes – one mounted on each side of the vehicle, and each powered by its relevant battery, as we fitted a dual battery split charge system.

1 Disconnect the battery earth lead(s). The first job you will need to do is run a heavy-duty cable (sufficient to carry the total current draw by all the circuits the fusebox will protect) from the positive terminal on the battery, through the bulkhead (use a grommet in any hole where the wires pass through the bulkhead) and to the area in the cabin where you will mount the fusebox. Use heat shrink to protect the connections.

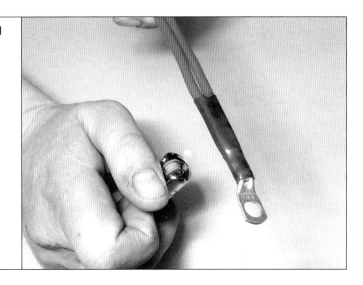

2 Cable tie the wires to the existing loom where possible so that they do not foul on moving or hot parts in the engine bay.

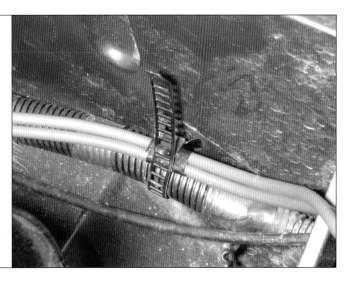

3 As the cable enters the vehicle, connect a ring terminal to the cable, and then on to one of the two posts on the junction box.

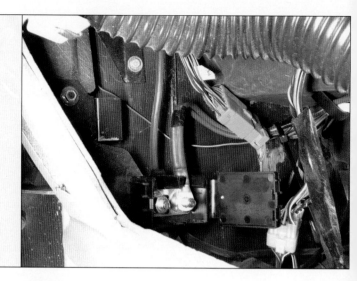

4 Using the shape of the fusebox as a template mark the area on the dash and cut out the hole.

5 Use a file or knife to remove any rough edges.

6 Fabricate a mounting plate so that you are able to mount the fusebox to the dash.

7 Fix eight separate wires (or however many terminals your fusebox has) to the remaining post on the junction box and feed through the hole you've just made in the dash . . .

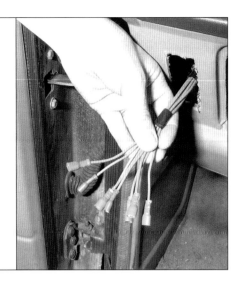

8 . . . where you can connect each of the wires to the connections on one side of the rear of the fusebox.

9 Screw the mounting plate and fusebox into place.

10 When a feed is required, ensure that the correctly rated fuse is fitted to the relevant pick up from the fusebox and refit the protective plastic cover. Make a note of which fuse protects which circuit for future reference, and keep it handy inside the car.

Nudge bar mounted lights

If at night you feel you could use a little more light in front of the vehicle, you may consider fitting some auxiliary driving lamps. These are normally fitted on the front bumper of your Discovery or on the nudge bar.

There are many different types of lamp available, ranging from budget priced units to high quality expensive items, so choose a lamp which best suits your pocket and lighting needs. It is a good idea to purchase lamps that come with plastic covers to protect the lenses when not in use.

There are various regulations about the positioning and use of auxiliary lights depending on their intended function (in fog, with dipped beam, with main beam …). The standard arrangement for driving lamps like these is to link them to the main beam circuit using a relay. See the wiring diagram for details.

The lamps we are fitting have a plastic outer body which protects against water ingress, and come complete with a plastic protective lens cover to be fitted when lamps are not in use.

1 Check out the wiring diagram to familiarise yourself with the circuit you now need to create.

Standard driving lamps

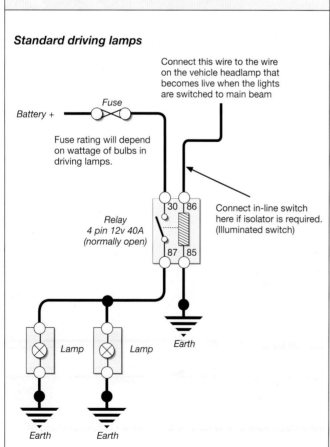

Connect this wire to the wire on the vehicle headlamp that becomes live when the lights are switched to main beam

Battery +

Fuse

Fuse rating will depend on wattage of bulbs in driving lamps.

Relay
4 pin 12v 40A
(normally open)

30 86

87 85

Connect in-line switch here if isolator is required. (Illuminated switch)

Lamp   Lamp

Earth

Earth   Earth

2 The lamps are bolted to the nudge bar through the pre-drilled mounting holes. Make sure the lamps are tightened securely and are correctly aligned.

3 If at any time you wish to remove the nudge bar it is sensible to do as we have done with our vehicle and create a set of connections just behind the front grille so that the wiring can be disconnected and the lamps removed more easily.

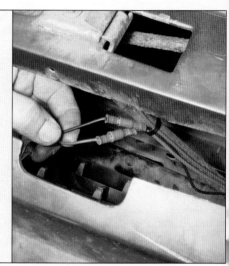

4 Remember to use good earth points and, if using the body of the vehicle as an earth, remove all traces of paint from the area using abrasive paper.

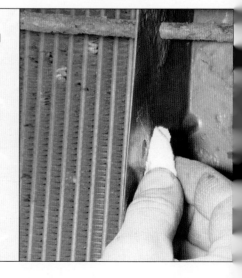

If you wish to add additional lighting to the front of your Discovery for night driving on or off road, one solution is to fit a bonnet pod with four driving lamps. A kit such as this will give you extra lights switched from main beam or independently if you desire, housed in a fibreglass pod which can be painted to match the colour of your vehicle. It is possible to switch the lamps on in pairs (inner and outer) or all at once, with or without main beam. In this instance we have chosen to switch our lamps in pairs (inner and outer) but they will only function whilst main beam is on and the light switch on the dash is on.

1 To reduce the risk of breakages in transit you may find that the lamps are not fitted to the pod, therefore the first job will be to assemble the light units. Begin by removing the backing plate

from each light that is held in place by a retaining screw, lift the bulb retaining clip and discard the plastic plug.

2 Fit the bulb assembly into the place and secure with the retaining clip.

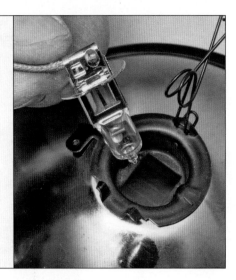

3 Using four lengths of suitable black wire crimp a spade connector to one end of each wire. Attach this connector to the earth post on the bulbholder assembly.

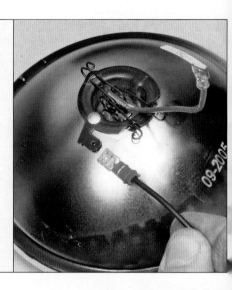

4 Take each of the four grommets supplied in the kit and slice into them using a sharp blade creating a means by which wiring can pass through.

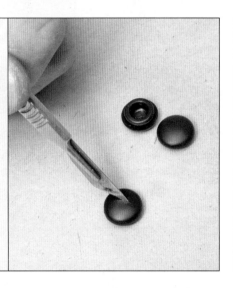

5 Fix the grommet to the pre-drilled hole in the backing plate and push the wires through. Then align and refit the backing plate to the lamp body.

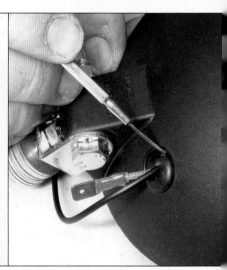

6 Remove a single washer and the retaining nut from the mounting bracket found at the base of each lamp. Place the lamp into the pre-drilled mounting hole on the pod, positioning the lamp centrally in the circular cut-out and flush with the outside edge of the pod. Holding the lamp in place, fit the washer and then tighten the retaining nut fully, but be careful not to overtighten.

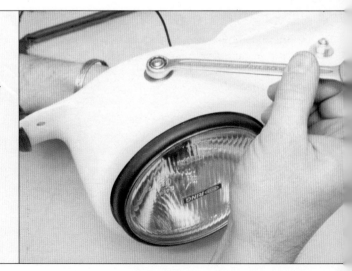

7 Next fully tighten the retaining nut that holds the lamp to the mounting bracket.

8 Once all four lamps are in place, position the pod centrally onto the bonnet.

9 Ask an assistant to press firmly on the pod holding it in place whilst two holes are drilled through the rear of the pod and bonnet. Space the two holes as far apart as possible, but allow for the size of the transparent washer against the edging trim. Before drilling check that the holes will miss areas of the bonnet that have been stiffened using double skinned metal and that the swarf generated will not fall into the engine bay.

10 The two Nyloc nuts, bolts, and metal and transparent washers are then used to secure the pod in place whilst you carry out the next stage.

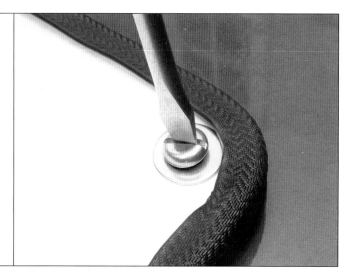

11 Drill the two front mounting holes now, choosing a suitable location for them as before – as far apart as possible and checking the area under the bonnet before drilling. Place the holes as far forward as possible on the pod to eliminate any movement between bonnet and pod. When the time comes, use the same fixings as above to secure the pod in place, although for now the pod must be removed from the vehicle.

12 Returning to the bonnet, drill a hole within the area that the pod will cover, large enough for 8 wires to pass through. Deburr any rough edges and fit a grommet to the hole.

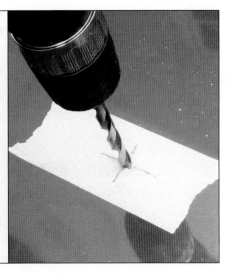

13 Lay out the loom supplied with the kit in the engine bay. Select the part of it that includes 2 white, 2 yellow and 4 black wires and, using some welding wire attached to the end of the wires, feed them up through the bonnet to the pod.

14 As the wires reach their destination the pod may be placed back on the bonnet for the final wiring-up stages. Don't forget the grommet!

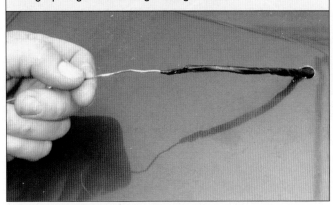

15 The four black wires from the loom are the earth wires to be connected to the black wire on the back of each of the lamps. The two yellow wires must be joined to the bulb wiring on the two outer lamps and the white wires joined to the bulb wiring on the inner lamps.

16 Next mount the two fuse/relay blocks from the loom to an appropriate area in the engine bay.

17 Take the single blue/white wire and tidily route that to the back of a headlight. Connect this to the main beam feed. Check your Haynes manual wiring diagrams for which colour wire that may be, as some models may differ from ours.

18 Take the switch wiring harness through the bulkhead to the dash and then on to wherever you plan to mount the switches (above the waterline if you do much wading). Connect one black wire to the earth side of each switch, the yellow wire to the live side of one switch and the black and white wire to the live side of the other. (These wire colours are just what we found in our kit, by the way. Yours may be different - read the instructions if in doubt.)

19 Finally back to the engine bay and connect the remaining black wire to a good earth in the engine bay and the red to the battery live. If you are fitting a split charge system use the auxiliary battery for this feed.

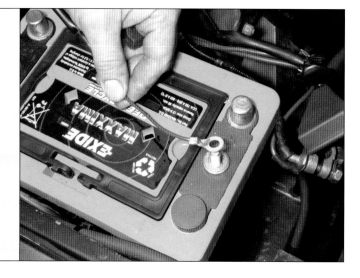

Headlamp protection grilles

Headlamp grilles offer protection to the vulnerable glass of the headlamp from all sorts of debris that can be thrown up by the vehicle on expedition, and particularly from branches and sticks in heavily-vegetated areas.

There are two types of headlamp protection on the market: a Perspex clear clip-on cover, or a metal grille. The clip-on cover is easy to fit and remove for cleaning purposes, inexpensive to buy, offers protection from road debris and vegetation but can crack if struck hard – still a cheaper option than a new headlight!

The metal grille is more of a permanent fixture designed to deflect stones and withstand heavier contact from branches and vegetation. The downside is that they can make cleaning the headlight glass more difficult. Some models feature hinges to facilitate cleaning.

The metal grille guards we are fitting to our project vehicle are available from Bearmach. We have chosen the style without hinges in a powder coated black finish.

1 Open the bonnet and remove the two screws securing the headlight trim panel in place, then repeat the process on the other side.

2 Offer and secure the grilles into position over the headlamp, using the two screws you have just removed.

3 If you then discover that the bottom mounting bracket doesn't slide into position under the front bumper where it should, because it is fouling on the headlight surround and the body underneath, use the following corrective measures to ensure a perfect fit . . .

4 . . . first, with the grille in position, mark the area that the bottom bracket covers on the front bumper and headlight surround using some masking tape.

5 Remove the grille and then the headlight surround from the vehicle (remember to unplug the wiring connector from the front indicators before lifting the trim away) and cut away the area of plastic the bracket is fouling on.

6 Now do the same to the offending area on the body that is now exposed.

7 Refit the headlight trim and then fit the grille in place as before. This time when sliding the bottom mounting bracket into place it should fit perfectly, so all that's left to do is tighten the two screws.

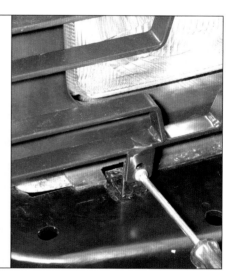

8 Repeat the whole process for the other side of the vehicle.

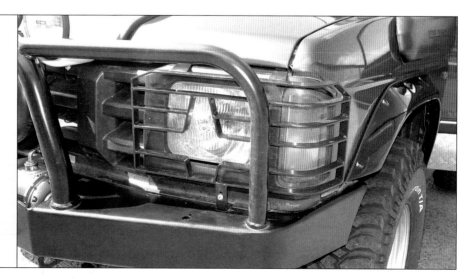

Rear light cluster protection grilles

As with the headlights, rear light protectors are available in two types: Perspex covers and metal grilles. Either will provide some protection against flying debris thrown up by your vehicle (or thrown at your vehicle by small boys in hostile territory), but they won't stop bullets or well-aimed rocks.

The protectors here are from Bearmach; there are plenty of others available, or if you're handy at metalwork you could always make your own.

1 Undo the fastener and remove the access panel to reveal the rear of the light cluster.

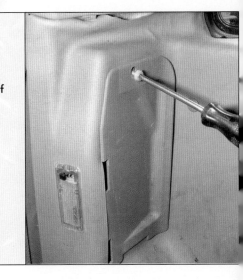

2 Remove the two retaining wing nuts that hold the unit in place.

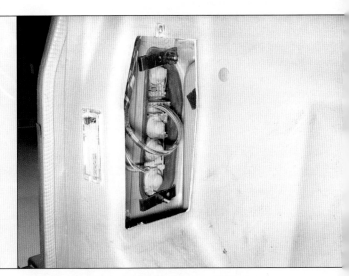

3 Gently withdraw the unit from the vehicle in order to gain better access for disconnecting the wiring plug. Once released, store the unit in a safe place, ie, not directly underfoot on the floor!

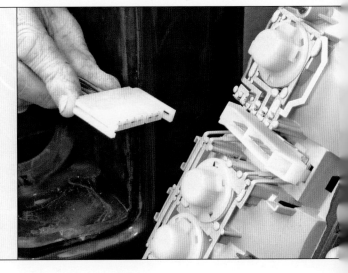

4 Take the self-adhesive foam strip supplied in the kit and affix to the light aperture on the vehicle. Once in place, remove the protective backing.

5 On a clean flat surface slide the light unit into place on the lamp guard.

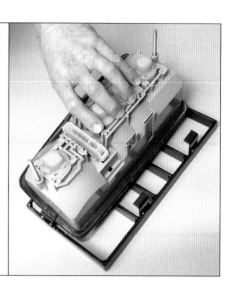

6 Place the light unit complete with new grille into the aperture of the vehicle, trapping the tabs on the grille between the gaskets. Reconnect the wiring plug.

7 Refit the two cluster retaining nuts and then the backing plate. Repeat the above process to the remaining light cluster.

Roof-mounted front lights

The key to any successful off-road vehicle is to equip it as best you can for any situation you may face. Roof-mounted lights, either on a roof rack or specifically designed bar, are of particular advantage for off-road driving for two main reasons:

- When crossing water sections lower level lamps should be turned off to avoid the coldness of the water cracking a hot headlamp lens or bulb.
- When travelling on rough surfaces at night, beams from a higher level can help depict how deep some potholes are on approach whereas a lower level spot lamp would simply send the light beam across the top of the track surface.

In this particular case we have chosen to fit 4x55W rectangular lights mounted on a bar that runs around the top edge of the windscreen. They will be switched from inside the cabin and be completely independent of any other lighting circuit.

1 To mount the bar, position it so that the ends lie flat in the rain gutter on either side of the vehicle. Find an assistant to hold the bar in place whilst the mounting holes are being drilled. Slot the drill bit into the pre-drilled holes on the bar (2 each side) and drill through the rain gutter.

2 Once the holes are drilled use nuts and bolts to hold the bar firmly in place. If the bolts you are using are too long simply remove the excess thread using a hacksaaw and deburr any rough edges.

3 The heads of the nuts and bolts can be painted black in order to blend in with the roof bar but we suggest you do this at the end of the procedure. Remove the bar from the vehicle and position it on a clean flat surface.

4 In the middle of each of the four light retaining brackets you will see a circular shape stamped into the metal. These act as a guide for drilling access holes to route the cables through, so drill them out now.

5 Decide which side you want the wiring to enter the cabin and drill one final hole in the bar on that side, large enough to accommodate the wiring, remembering to deburr all edges after. No wiring is supplied with this kit so ensure the cabling you are using is sufficient for this job.

6 There are several ways of physically wiring this bar up so decide the way you are most confident with – refer to the wiring diagram for more information. Route the wiring (a live and earth) to each of the four lights. Starting with the furthest bracket away, bare approximately an inch of wire and push the cable into the bar until you can see it arrive at the access hole of the bracket. Use a piece of welding rod bent round to form a hook to grab at the wires from inside the bar.

7 Once this has been completed you should have something that looks a little bit like this.

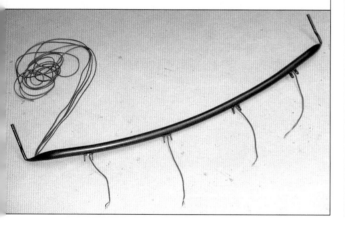

8 Offer the bar into place once more and ask an assistant to hold it in place whilst you mark the location of an access hole large enough for the wires to run through into the cab.

9 Before drilling the access hole remove the bar from the vehicle. After drilling, to offer a degree of protection to the wires, fit a grommet to the hole.

10 On a clean flat surface, take the first light and remove the two screws from plastic surround. The light unit then comes apart in 3 sections.

11 Thread the wire from the bar through the hole found on the rear of the plastic light casing. Protect the wire by fitting a grommet to the hole at the same time. The casing can then be bolted to the bar.

12 Remove a few inches of the insulation surrounding the two wires and crimp a female spade connector to each one.

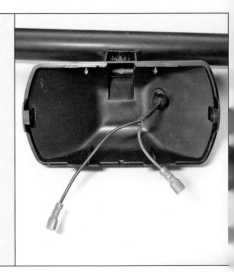

13 Select the light unit itself and remove the bulbholder by unclipping the retaining clip. Check that there is a bulb present, then refit. **Note:** *When handling the new bulb, use a tissue or clean cloth to avoid touching the glass with the fingers; moisture and grease from the skin can cause blackening and rapid failure of the bulb. If the glass is accidentally touched, wipe it clean using methylated spirit.*

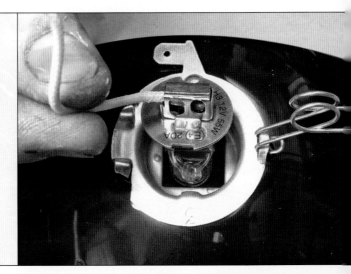

14 Take the black wire and fix it to the earth terminal post.

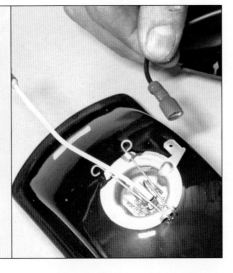

15 Then place the protective plastic sleeve supplied in the kit over the live wire from the bulb and make the connection with the live female spade connector.

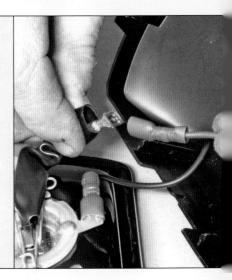

16 Rebuild the light unit and refit the retaining screws. Now repeat steps 10 onwards until all four lights are mounted to the bar.

17 The light bar can be mounted in place permanently and the wiring routed into the cabin for the final stages of this procedure.

18 Check out the wiring diagram for more information on how to wire the relay and switch in. Ensure that switch is positioned in a convenient place in the cabin, close to the driver for ease of use.

Roof mounted spot lamps

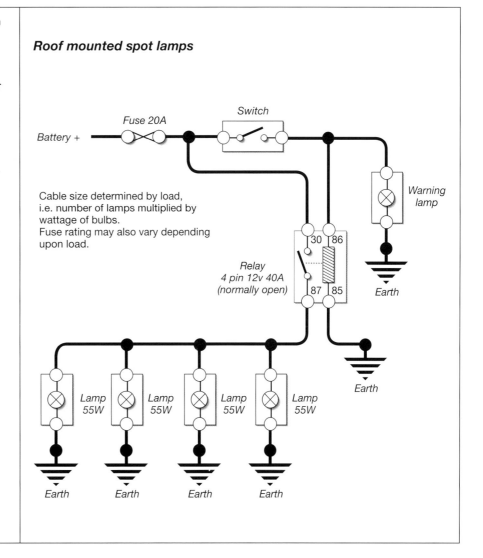

Cable size determined by load, i.e. number of lamps multiplied by wattage of bulbs.
Fuse rating may also vary depending upon load.

Roof-mounted rear working light

Remember that whilst having sufficient lighting on the front of your vehicle is essential, it is equally important for the rear as well, particularly if you operate a rear winch or need access to tools and jacks stored on the roof rack or in the luggage area. Here we show you how to fit a waterproof plug manufactured by Durite. The beauty about this particular style of plug is that the light unit can be removed at anytime by simply unplugging it from the roof and refitting the protective cap – this is ideal if your work light is mounted on a roof rack that may need to be removed from time to time. For ease of operation a switch is mounted inside the cabin so the light can be operated when needed by the driver.

1 Firstly chose the location of your work light – somewhere fairly close to the rear of the vehicle and in area that it won't be fouled by a roof rack. Once you've decided, mark the areas for drilling the mounting holes by using the plug as a template.

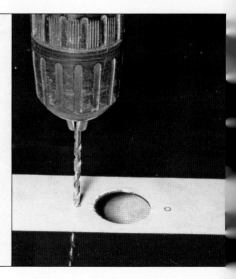

2 As you've probably already guessed the next step is to drill the hole and as always deburr those sharp edges. Remember to fit a rubber grommet to the metal roof.

3 Take a live feed using suitable cable from a source such as the auxiliary fusebox or direct from the battery with an in-line fuse, and run it to a switch mounted on the dashboard. Check the current rating of the switch and be aware that there must be a warning tell-tale illuminated when the light is on. **Note:** *The wiring in of a relay is also recommended for this procedure.*

Rear single work lamp

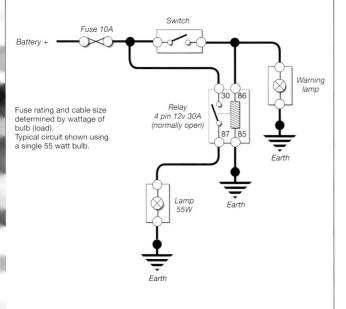

Fuse rating and cable size determined by wattage of bulb (load).
Typical circuit shown using a single 55 watt bulb.

Battery +

Fuse 10A

Switch

*Relay
4 pin 12v 30A
(normally open)*

30 86
87 85

*Warning
lamp*

Earth

Earth

*Lamp
55W*

Earth

4 From the relay run the live wire to the back of the vehicle, tidily routing it under trim panels and headlining until it reaches the base of the plug where it will be threaded through the plastic sleeve then connected to one of the pins.

5 To complete the circuit, an earth wire is attached to one of the two remaining pins (the third is not required) and then routed back inside the vehicle to an earth. Don't forget that when wiring the corresponding plug to the work light you use the same two pins.

6 Push the plastic sleeve into place on the plug and screw the whole assembly into place.

7 When you need light, just plug the lamp in and switch it on.

CB radio installation

Whether travelling alone or in the company of other vehicles, it is a good idea to have some sort of communication fitted to your vehicle. Whether it is to keep in touch with the rest of the convoy or summon emergency help, a CB radio is certainly a low cost option to bear in mind. Before using such equipment however, it is important to keep on the right side of the law and apply for the correct licence for your equipment from the Post Office – it is illegal to transmit without a licence. Once legal, installation can begin.

The CB radio kit that we sourced locally did not include an antenna, antenna lead or mounting bracket, so be aware that you may have the same problem.

External Contractors

The Radiocommunications Agency has appointed an external contractor to issue and renew CB Radio Licences. The external contractor is:

The Radio Licensing Centre (RLC)
PO Box 885
Bristol BS99 5LG
Tel: 01179 258333

CB radio licences have been contracted out because they are easy to issue, and do not require specialist knowledge or co-ordination, and also for more cost-effective issue than under the previous system, ie, applying through the Post office.

1 The process of fitting a CB radio is straightforward. Firstly decide where to mount the unit and fabricate a mounting plate for it if necessary.

2 Next you need to decide how you will route the wires from the dash to an area where you can source a fused live and earth. It may be necessary to remove the instrument cluster (refer to your Haynes manual) and drill a hole in the dash for this.

3 With the hole drilled, the live and earth wire can be routed under the dash, through the bulkhead and towards the main battery in the

engine bay to pick up a live and earth feed. An auxiliary fusebox, if fitted, is also equally acceptable for the required live feed, and earth the other lead to an earth point on the body. **Note:** *Better performance is gained if the leads connect directly to the battery, as the battery will act as a natural suppressor and stop any alternator whine that may be present.*

4 The antenna cable is routed from the antenna on the roof, down the A-pillar and under the dash to the base of the unit, so all that's left to do is push the antenna lead into place and secure.

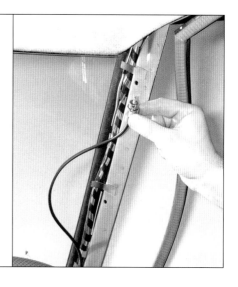

5 Affix the CB unit to its own mounting bracket . . .

6 . . . then fit the entire unit to the plate you fabricated earlier.

7 Next decide on a suitable location to mount the microphone. Mark, then drill the holes and secure the microphone bracket in place with two self-tapping screws. Make sure the trailing cable will not hinder any operation of the vehicle.

8 Slide the microphone into place on the bracket.

9 Then simply push the cable from the microphone into place on the CB unit.

10 It is possible to source an additional speaker that will plug into the radio unit. They come complete with a mounting bracket and can be mounted anywhere you wish – particularly in areas where extra sound is more useful, ie, near the driver!

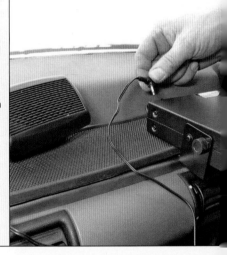

11 Finally, with the wiring fed through the bulkhead, it arrives at the battery. The live wire has an in-line fuse already fitted so it can be attached to the positive terminal of the battery using a ring terminal. This supply must be fused to maintain electrical safety. Complete the circuit by attaching the black to the negative terminal of the battery. Then you can get out the instruction book and learn all about the channels and how to use your CB radio properly!

Mounting the antenna

Start by deciding where to mount the antenna – there are many different locations you can chose from on the vehicle and a range of brackets available to buy to ensure that it's mounted safely and securely. Make sure that wherever you mount the antenna it won't get in the way of a roof rack, or roof-mounted lights. Two of the most popular mounting locations (roof and rain gutter) are shown below, including showing how to fit different types of antenna bases.

Rain-gutter mounted antenna base

This type of antenna base is specifically designed to fit areas such as the rain gutter or roof rack. They are fairly inexpensive to buy and provide a neat finish, however be aware that on off-road vehicles an antenna mounted to the side of a vehicle may be vulnerable to branches and other obstacles in its path. See the section on *Bush wires* to help overcome this potential problem.

1 Firstly offer the mounting bracket into place to check for fitment.

2 The bracket affixes to the gutter by two screws that, when tightened, act like clamps. The assembly is designed to tilt forward and back to facilitate access to the bolts.

3 Place the main body of the bracket in an upright position then tighten in place using an Allen key.

4 Screw the antenna into place on the base.

5 Finally route the wire down the gutter towards the front of the car. A second hole will need to be drilled into the roof or body of the vehicle at a convenient point for the cable to enter the cabin and then routed to the rear of the CB radio set. **Note:** *It is possible to route the cable around a door weather seal, but be aware this may cause water leaks due to insufficient pressure all around the seal.*

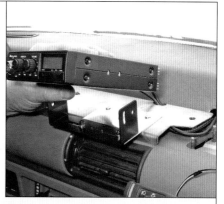

Roof-mounted antenna base No 1

1 Firstly find the centre point of the roof and mark the position for drilling – use masking tape. Check that the position you've  chosen does not interfere with any existing wiring or facia panels inside the vehicle. It is possible to mount the antenna so that, by removing the front overhead switch panel inside the vehicle, you access the base. This saves damaging the headlining in any way and does not leave you with unsightly wiring on show. Remember to clean the area around the hole on the inside using some emery paper to remove the paint, this will ensure a good earth for the antenna.

2 With the hole drilled, push the antenna base down into place and move to the inside of the vehicle for the next step.

3 Remove the overhead facia panel to get access to the base of the antenna.

4 Fit the triangular washer followed by a star washer followed by retaining nut to complete the assembly. The fitting kit was supplied with the base, so bear in mind that our kit may differ to yours.

5 Last job here is to fit the antenna lead supplied with the base kit into place on the base and route the wire down the A-pillar to the main CB unit.

6 The final job to be done is screw the antenna into place and the task is completed.

Roof-mounted antenna base No 2

1 Repeat step 1 as above. Once the hole has been drilled, move inside the vehicle. Using some emery paper remove the paint around the hole, this will ensure a good earth for the antenna.

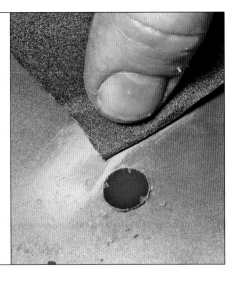

2 Push the antenna base, complete with washer, up through the mounting hole in the roof.

3 You may require an assistant to hold the base in place from inside the vehicle whilst the rubber washer and antenna adapter are fitted. Tighten the adapter fully with a spanner.

4 Once the antenna has been screwed into place move to the inside of the vehicle.

5 Fit the antenna lead into place on the base and route the wire down the A-pillar to the main CB unit.

Distance/trip meter

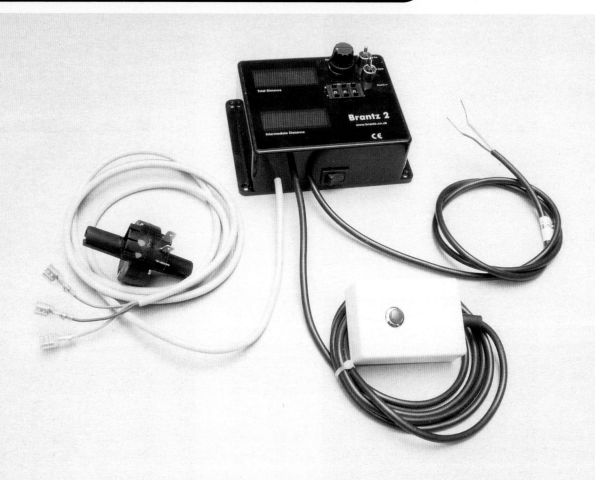

Off-road navigation can be made much easier if you fit a distance or trip meter to your vehicle, especially if you compete in events using road books. On a European event such as the Belgian National, distances given between points are in kilometres or tenths of, and most Discoveries have their odometers calibrated in miles, so this can get very confusing. A correctly calibrated distance meter will make this task much simpler. Calibration of the Brantz meter we fitted to our vehicle is quite straightforward, but it should be noted that if the tyre size or gearing is changed after calibration it will be necessary to repeat the procedure.

To calibrate the unit you will need an accurately measured kilometre on a quiet stretch of road. Drive the measured kilometre and note the three-digit figure on the readout. This is the calibration figure for your vehicle with its current gearing and tyres. All you need to do is to enter this number into the thumbwheel switches and you are ready to use the unit.

Fitment is fairly straightforward, however, the standard

inductive pickup supplied for use on the speedometer cable is unsuitable for use on a Discovery due to the nature of the cable, so an alternative pickup is required.

1 Decide on a suitable location within the cabin to mount the trip meter and fabricate a mounting plate. Drill two holes in the plate to route the wiring through. Remember to fit grommets to any holes that wiring passes through.

2 Pass the two separate wiring cables through the holes. The white cable with three wires – blue, green and brown – will be connected to the inductive pick up. The black cable containing the brown and green/yellow wires will connect to a live supply and earth.

3 Bolt the trip meter to the mounting plate . . .

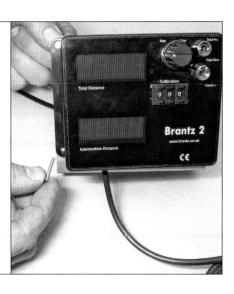

4 . . . then bolt the whole assembly to the area on the dash where you've decided to mount it permanently. We have had a custom-made alloy plate built across the top of the dashboard which means we can bolt items to it, whilst routing wires tidily out of sight under it, and down to the footwell areas which are ideal for picking up live and earth feeds from the main or auxiliary fuseboxes. To start with, the white cable will be routed towards the driver's footwell.

5 The black cable heads to our auxiliary fusebox, conveniently situated on the dash to pick up a live feed (see *Auxiliary fusebox* section).

6 The brown wire will be connected to the live feed on the fusebox. There are many earth points in this area for the green/yellow wire to be connected to.

7 A 2 amp fuse must be placed in the holder for this circuit. Make a note of which fuse in the box serves which circuit for reference later.

8 In the original kit we were supplied with a universal speedometer cable sensor but when attempts to fit this to our speedo proved futile, we had to go back to the manufacturer and ask them to supply us with a wheel sensor instead. The wheel sensor comes complete with cable. The next job here is to create yet another mounting plate to bolt this sensor to. We have chosen to fix the plate to the front diff guard (or standard bracket if front diff guard is not fitted) and pick up the 'triggers' from L-shaped brackets, which we will attach to the four prop shaft bolts. As an alternative this could be fitted in the same way to the handbrake drum on the rear prop shaft.

9 Using L-shaped brackets available from most DIY centres, attach one bracket to each of the four flange bolts on the front prop shaft. They may require some trimming to fit and mounting holes drilled in one end.

10 Fit the wheel sensor to the mounting plate.

11 Using feeler blades, ensure that there is exactly 1 mm of clearance between each of the brackets and sensor. Slacken the bolts and reposition as necessary, then tighten the bolts to the specified torque. Once this has been done, route the cable tidily up into the driver's footwell where it is connected to the cable from the trip meter. **Note:** *Take a few moments to familiarise yourself with the operating instructions and the procedure for calibrating the trip meter. You will need to calibrate the meter before use.*

Available on the market today are more and more varieties of satellite navigational equipment. The majority of these self-contained units are of street-level mapping only, which is fine if you are using normal roads as they will more often than not guide you to your chosen destination with the minimum of fuss.

For off-road mapping you will require something a little different. It is possible to buy mapping data (at Ordnance Survey level) suitable for download onto a laptop computer or PDA. With this system you have a scrolling map, your position pinpointed by a GPS receiver connected to your laptop or PDA via a Bluetooth connection. By using this type of system you are able to plan your routes easily using 3D mapping or aerial photography and build a database of your favourite lanes, or use to retrace your steps if necessary.

Most areas are available to buy, just the same as purchasing a hard-copy Ordnance Survey map. This digital version means that you'll never find yourself asking 'where are we now?' because the GPS receiver will instantly show you your position. A very neat on/off-road navigational solution indeed!

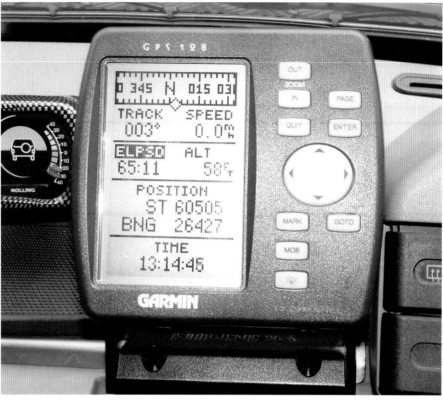

Aerial

Satellite navigation systems require a separate aerial to receive the satellite's signal.

There are four basic types of aerials available:

- Adhesive (glass-mounted) – adhesive secures the aerial to the outside glass and the wire is attached inside the window by a coupler.
- Adhesive (roof-mounted) – adhesive permanently secures the aerial to the vehicle, the wires must then be routed into the vehicle.
- Magnetic (roof-mounted) – similar to the adhesive type mentioned above, but this style can be easily removed from the vehicle when required.
- Mast type – these types of aerials are installed primarily on large trucks and lorries.

The aerial must be mounted in a position where it can 'see' the GPS satellites without sheet metal getting in the way. On the roof or on the outside of the glass is ideal. In areas of good reception you can also get an acceptable result with the aerial mounted inside the vehicle on the dash or rear parcel shelf so that it can receive a signal through the glass.

In most cases the aerial is matched to its cable length, so do not shorten or extend the cable. Secure any excess cable in wide loops - don't coil it up, as this too may affect aerial performance.

Professional mechanics are trained in safe working procedures. However enthusiastic you may be about getting on with the job at hand, take the time to ensure that your safety is not put at risk. A moment's lack of attention can result in an accident, as can failure to observe simple precautions.

There will always be new ways of having accidents, and the following is not a comprehensive list of all dangers; it is intended rather to make you aware of the risks and to encourage a safe approach to all work you carry out on your vehicle.

Asbestos

- Certain friction, insulating, sealing and other products – such as brake pads, clutch linings, gaskets, etc. – may contain asbestos. Extreme care must be taken to avoid inhalation of dust from such products since it is hazardous to health. If in doubt, assume that they do contain asbestos.

Fire

- Remember at all times that fuel is highly flammable. Never smoke or have any kind of naked flame around, when working on the vehicle. But the risk does not end there – a spark caused by an electrical short-circuit, by two metal surfaces contacting each other, by careless use of tools, or even by static electricity built up in your body under certain conditions, can ignite fuel vapour, which in a confined space is highly explosive. Never use petrol as a cleaning solvent. Use an approved safety solvent.
- Always disconnect the battery earth terminal before working on any part of the fuel or electrical system, and never risk spilling fuel on to a hot engine or exhaust.
- It is recommended that a fire extinguisher of a type suitable for fuel and electrical fires is kept handy in the garage or workplace at all times. Never try to extinguish a fuel or electrical fire with water.

Fumes

- Certain fumes are highly toxic and can quickly cause unconsciousness and even death if inhaled to any extent. Fuel vapour comes into this category, as do the vapours from certain solvents such as trichloro-ethylene. Any draining or pouring of such volatile fluids should be done in a well ventilated area.
- When using cleaning fluids and solvents, read the instructions carefully. Never use materials from unmarked containers – they may give off poisonous vapours.
- Never run the engine of a motor vehicle in an enclosed space such as a garage. Exhaust fumes contain carbon monoxide which is extremely poisonous; if you need to run

the engine, always do so in the open air or at least have the rear of the vehicle outside the workplace.

The battery

- Never cause a spark, or allow a naked light near the vehicle's battery. It will normally be giving off a certain amount of hydrogen gas, which is highly explosive.
- Always disconnect the battery ground (earth) terminal before working on the fuel or electrical systems (except where noted).
- On conventional fillable batteries, loosen the filler plugs or cover when charging the battery from an external source. Do not charge at an excessive rate or the battery may burst.
- Take care when topping up (fillable batteries), cleaning or carrying the battery. The acid electrolyte, even when diluted, is very corrosive and should not be allowed to contact the eyes or skin. Always wear rubber gloves and goggles or a face shield. If you ever need to prepare electrolyte yourself, always add the acid slowly to the water; never add the water to the acid.

Electricity

- When using an electric power tool, inspection light etc., always ensure that the appliance is correctly connected to its plug and that, where necessary, it is properly earthed. Do not use such appliances in damp conditions and, again, beware of creating a spark or applying excessive heat in the vicinity of fuel or fuel vapour. Also ensure that the appliances meet national safety standards.
- A severe electric shock can result from touching certain parts of the electrical system, such as the spark plug wires (HT leads), when the engine is running, particularly if components are damp or the insulation is defective. Where an electronic ignition system is used, the secondary (HT) voltage is much higher and could prove fatal.

Crushing

- Having your vehicle land on top of you is no laughing matter, and it's a nasty accident waiting to happen if you risk using dodgy old jacks, bricks, and other means of lifting/supporting your vehicle. Please don't.
- Your standard vehicle jack is for emergency roadside use only – a proper trolley jack and a set of axle stands is essential, and might save broken bones. Don't buy a cheap trolley jack, and don't expect a well-used secondhand one to be perfect, either – when the hydraulic seals start to fail, a trolley jack will drop very fast; this is why you should always have decent axle stands in place under the vehicle as well.

Steering, suspension & brakes

- Badly fitted modifications in these areas could land you and others in hospital or worse. Enough said. It's always worth getting a friend, or a professional garage, to check over what you've just fitted (or even what you've just had fitted, in some cases – not all 'pro' fitters are perfect!). Pay attention to tightening vital nuts and bolts properly – buy or borrow a torque wrench.
- To be absolutely sure, take your behicle to an MOT tester – this man's your ultimate authority on safety, after all.
- Even properly-fitted modifications can radically alter the vehiclo's handling and not always for the better. Take a few days getting used to how the vehicle feels before showing off.

Wheels

- Don't take liberties fitting wheels. Make sure the wheels have the right stud/bolt hole pattern for your vehicle, and that the wheel nuts/bolts are doing their job. Bolts which are too long might catch on your brakes – too short, and, well, the wheels are just waiting to fall off. Also pay attention to the bolt heads or wheel nuts – some are supposed to have large tapered washers fitted, to locate properly in the wheel. If the nuts/bolts 'pull through' the wheel when tightened, then the wheel will fall off.

Airbags

Take care not to tap into the airbag wiring to run any extra electrical kit. Any modifications to the airbag circuit could set it off unexpectedly.

Remember...

- Don't start the engine without first ascertaining that the transmission is in neutral.
- Don't suddenly remove the pressure cap from a hot cooling system – cover it with a cloth and release the pressure gradually first, or you may get scalded by escaping coolant.
- Don't attempt to drain oil until you are sure it has cooled sufficiently to avoid scalding you.
- Don't grasp any part of the engine or exhaust system without first ascertaining that it is cool enough not to burn you.
- Don't allow brake fluid or antifreeze to contact the vehicle's paintwork or plastic components.
- Don't syphon toxic liquids such as fuel, hydraulic fluid or antifreeze by mouth, or allow them to remain on your skin.
- Don't inhale dust – it may be injurious to health (see *Asbestos* heading).
- Don't allow any spilled oil or grease to remain on the floor – wipe it up right away, before someone slips on it.
- Don't use ill-fitting spanners or other tools which may slip and cause injury.
- Don't lift a heavy component which may be beyond your capability – get assistance.
- Don't rush to finish a job or take unverified short cuts.
- Don't allow children or animals in or around an unattended vehicle.
- Don't inflate a tyre above the recommended pressure. Apart from overstressing the carcass, in extreme cases the tyre may blow off forcibly.
- Do ensure that the vehicle is supported securely when the vehicle is blocked up to aid wheel removal.
- Do take care when attempting to loosen a stubborn nut or bolt.
- Do wear eye protection when using power tools such as drill, sander, bench grinder etc.
- Do use a barrier cream on your hands prior to undertaking dirty jobs – it will protect your skin from infection as well as making the dirt easier to remove afterwards; but make sure your hands aren't left slippery. Note that long-term contact with used engine oil can be a health hazard.
- Do keep loose clothing (cuffs, ties etc. and long hair) well out of the way of moving mechanical parts.
- Do remove rings, wristwatch etc., before working on the vehicle – especially the electrical system.
- Do keep your work area tidy – it is only too easy to fall over articles left lying around.
- Do exercise caution when compressing springs for removal or installation. Ensure that the tension is applied and released in a controlled manner, using suitable tools which preclude the possibility of the spring escaping violently.
- Do ensure that any lifting tackle used has a safe working load rating adequate for the job.
- Do get someone to check periodically that all is well, when working alone on the vehicle.
- Do carry out work in a logical sequence and check that everything is correctly assembled and tightened afterwards.
- Do remember that your vehicle's safety affects that of yourself and others. If in doubt on any point, get professional advice.
- If in spite of following these precautions, you are unfortunate enough to injure yourself, seek medical attention as soon as possible.

The harsh & painful truth

The minute you start down the road to a modified vehicle, you stand a chance of being in trouble with the law.

There are vehicle-related regulations called Construction & Use. It's a huge set of books, used by the vehicle manufacturers and the Department of Transport among others, and it sets out in black and white all the legal issues that could land you in trouble. It's the ultimate authority for modifying, in theory. But few people know all of it inside-out, and it's forever being updated and revised, so it's not often enforced to the letter at the roadside – just in court. Despite the existence of C & U, in trying to put together any guide to the law and modifying, it quickly becomes clear that almost everything's a 'grey area', with no-one prepared to go on record and say what is okay to modify and what's not. So if there's no fixed rules (in the real world), how are you meant to live by them? In the circumstances, all we can try to do is help to make some sense of this.

Avoiding roadside interviews

Why do some people get pulled all the time, and others hardly ever? It's often all about attitude.

The worst thing from your point of view is that, once you've been stopped, it's down to that particular policeman's judgement as to whether your vehicle is illegal. If you can persuade him/her that you're at least taking on board what's being said, you might be let off with a warning. If it goes further, you'll be reported for an offence – while this doesn't mean you'll end up being prosecuted for it, it isn't good. Some defects (like worn tyres) will possibly result in a 'seven-day wonder', which usually means you have to fix whatever's deemed wrong, maybe get the vehicle inspected, and present yourself with the proof at a police station inside seven days, or face prosecution.

If you can drive reasonably sensibly, and can ideally show that you've tried to keep your vehicle legal when you get questioned, you stand a much better chance of enjoying your relationship with your vehicle. This guide is intended to help you steer clear of the more obvious things you could get pulled for. By reading it, you might even be able to have an informed, well-mannered discussion about things legal with the next officer of the law you meet at the side of the road. As in: 'Oh really, officer? I was not aware of that. Thank you for pointing it out.' Just don't argue with them, that's all...

Documents

The first thing you'll be asked to produce. If you're driving around without tax, MOT or insurance, we might as well stop now, as you won't be doing much more driving of anything after just one pull.

Okay, so you don't normally carry all your vehicle-related documents with you – most people keep them safely at home. But carrying photocopies of your licence, MOT and insurance certificate is a good idea. While they're not legally-binding absolute proof, producing these in a roadside check may possibly mean you don't have to produce the real things at a police station later in the week. It shows a certain responsibility and confidence in your own legality on the road, too.

Number plates

One of the simplest modifications, and one of the easiest to spot (and prove). Nowadays, any changes made to the standard approved character font (such as italics or fancy type), spacing, or size of the plate constitutes an offence. Remember too that if you've moved the rear plate from its original spot it still has to be properly lit at night. You're unlikely to even buy an illegal plate now, as the companies making them are also liable for prosecution if you get stopped

It's all just something else to blame on speed cameras – plates have to be easy for them to shoot.

While this offence only entails a small fine and confiscation of the plates, you could be drawing unwelcome police attention to the rest of your vehicle.

Sunstrips and tints

The sunstrip is now a popular item. The sunstrip should not be so low down the screen that it interferes with your ability to see out. As a guide, if the strip's so low your wiper(s) touch it, it's too low. Window tinting is a trickier area. It seems you can have up to a 25% tint on a windscreen, and up to 30% on all other glass – but measuring this is difficult. And what do you do if your glass is tinted to start with? – probably nothing!

Of course you can buy window film in various 'darknesses', from not-very-dark to 'ambulance-black', but being able to buy it does not make it legal for road use (most companies cover themselves by saying 'for show use only'). Go for just a light smoke on the side and rear glass, and you'd have to be unlucky to get done for it. If you must fit really dark tints, you're safest doing the rear side windows only.

Some police forces now have a light meter to test light transmission through glass at the roadside – fail this, and it's a big on-the-spot fine.

Lights

Lights of all kinds have to be one of the single biggest problem areas in modifying, and the police are well-informed.

First of all, don't bother with any lights which aren't fully UK-legal – it's just too much hassle. Being 'E-marked' only makes them legal in Europe, and most of Europe drives on the right. Some european style lights have left-hand-drive rear clusters, and as a result, have no rear reflectors and a rear foglight on the wrong side.

Once you've had any headlight modifications done always have the beam alignment checked – it's part of the MOT, after all. The same applies to any front fogs or spots you've fitted (the various points of law involved here are too many to mention – light colour, height, spacing, operation with main/dipped headlights – ask at an MOT centre before fitting, and have them checked out after fitting).

The police might even question the legality of the new blue headlight bulbs – are they too powerful? Keeping the bulb packaging in the glovebox might be a neat solution here (60/55W max).

Big wheels/tyres

Make sure the wheels don't rub on, or stick out from, the arches – either of these will prove to be a problem if you get stopped.

Exhausts

One of the easiest-to-fit performance upgrades. Unless your chosen pipe/system is just too loud, you'd be very unlucky to get stopped for it, but if you will draw attention this way, you could be kicking yourself later. It is possible you may get stopped for a random roadside emissions check.

It's also worth mentioning that your tailpipe mustn't stick out beyond the very back of the vehicle, or in any other way which might be dangerous to pedestrians.

Seats and harnesses

Have to meet the UK safety standards, and must be securely bolted in. It should be possible to fasten and release any seat belt or harness with one hand. Given that seat belts are pretty important safety features, it's understandable then that the police don't like to see flimsy strut braces used as seat harness mounting points. Any other signs of bodging will also spell trouble. It's unlikely they'd bother with a full safety inspection at the roadside, but they could insist on a full MOT test/engineer's report inside 7 days.

Other mods

We'll never cover everything else here, and the law's always changing anyway, but here goes with some other legalistic points we've noted on the way:

a All except the most prehistoric vehicles must have at least one rear foglight. If there's only one, it must be fitted on the right. We've never heard of anyone getting stopped for it, but you must also have a pair of rear reflectors.

b Fuel filler caps have to be fitted so there's no danger of fuel spillage, or of excess fumes leaking from the top of the filler neck.

c You have to have at least one exterior mirror, and it must be capable of being adjusted somehow.

d If you fit new fog and spotlights, they actually have to work. No-one fits new lights just for show, but if they stop working later when a fuse blows, relay packs up, or the wiring connectors rust up, you'd better fix 'em or remove 'em.

Any questions? Try the MOT Helpline (0845 6005977).

Thanks to . . .

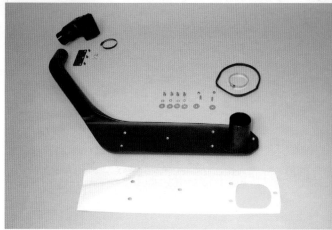

Bearmach plc
www.bearmach.com
02920 856550

Scorpion Racing Ltd
www.scorpion-racing.co.uk
02082 114888

Hi Clones
www.damdesign.com
01525 223083

Twisted Performance
www.twistedperformance.co.uk
08458 909909

Devon 4 x 4
www.devon4x4.com
01769 550900

Don Barrow Rally Navigation
www.donbarrow.co.uk
01625 429092

Overland Expedition Company
www.oec4x4.com
01626 356555

The 4 x 4 Store - Exeter
www.exeter4x4.co.uk
01404 850166

With thanks to:
Mike Webb for the loan of the
vehicle

Tony (Too Tall) Nicholls

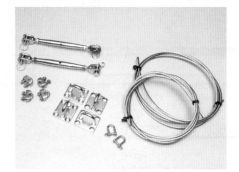

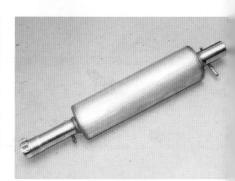

Other books of interest from Haynes Publishing

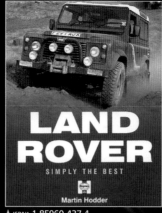

LAND ROVER
SIMPLY THE BEST
Martin Hodder
ISBN: 1 85960 437 4

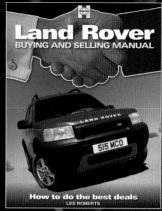

Land Rover
BUYING AND SELLING MANUAL
How to do the best deals
LES ROBERTS
ISBN: 1 84425 336 8

you&your
Land Rover Discovery
Dave Pollard | Buying, enjoying, maintaining, modifying
ISBN: 1 85960 683 0

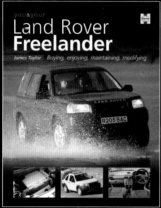

you&your
Land Rover Freelander
James Taylor | Buying, enjoying, maintaining, modifying
ISBN: 1 85960 899 X

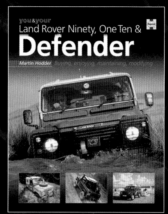

you&your
Land Rover Ninety, One Ten &
Defender
Martin Hodder | Buying, enjoying, maintaining, modifying
ISBN: 1 85960 667 9

you&your
Range Rover
Dave Pollard | Buying, enjoying, maintaining, modifying
ISBN: 1 85960 617 2

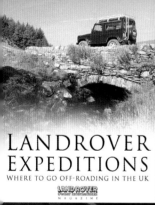

LANDROVER EXPEDITIONS
WHERE TO GO OFF-ROADING IN THE UK
LAND ROVER OWNER International MAGAZINE
ISBN: 1 84425 141 1

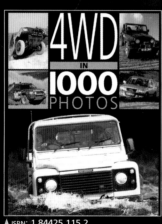

4WD IN 1000 PHOTOS
ISBN: 1 84425 115 2

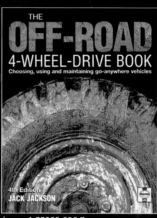

THE **OFF-ROAD**
4-WHEEL-DRIVE BOOK
Choosing, using and maintaining go-anywhere vehicles
4th Edition
JACK JACKSON
ISBN: 1 85960 606 7

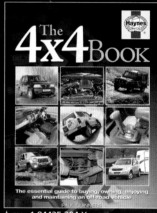

The **4x4** BOOK
The essential guide to buying, owning, enjoying and maintaining an off-road vehicle
PAUL GUINNESS
ISBN: 1 84425 304 X

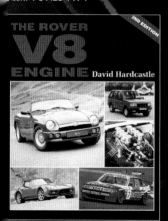

THE ROVER **V8 ENGINE** David Hardcastle
2ND EDITION
ISBN: 0 85429 961 0

TUNING ROVER **V8** ENGINES
How to get the best performance for road and competition use
David Hardcastle
ISBN: 0 85429 933 5

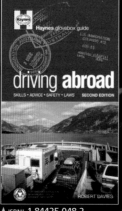

Haynes glovebox guide
driving abroad
SKILLS • ADVICE • SAFETY • LAWS   SECOND EDITION
ROBERT DAVIES
ISBN: 1 84425 048 2

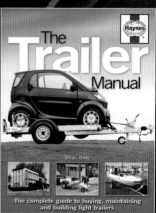

The **Trailer** Manual
Brian Bate
The complete guide to buying, maintaining and building light trailers
ISBN: 1 84425 212 4

Haynes Car Manuals

Title	No.
Alfa Romeo Alfasud/Sprint (74 - 88) up to F *	0292
Alfa Romeo Alfetta (73 - 87) up to E *	0531
Audi 80, 90 & Coupe Petrol (79 - Nov 88) up to F	0605
Audi 80, 90 & Coupe Petrol (Oct 86 - 90) D to H	1491
Audi 100 & 200 Petrol (Oct 82 - 90) up to H	0907
Audi 100 & A6 Petrol & Diesel (May 91 - May 97) H to P	3504
Audi A3 Petrol & Diesel (96 - May 03) P to 03	4253
Audi A4 Petrol & Diesel (95 - Feb 00) M to V	3575
Austin A35 & A40 (56 - 67) up to F *	0118
Austin/MG/Rover Maestro 1.3 & 1.6 Petrol (83 - 95) up to M	0922
Austin/MG Metro (80 - May 90) up to G	0718
Austin/Rover Montego 1.3 & 1.6 Petrol (84 - 94) A to L	1066
Austin/Rover Montego 2.0 Petrol (84 - 95) A to M	1067
Mini (59 - 69) up to H *	0527
Mini (69 - 01) up to X	0646
Austin/Rover 2.0 litre Diesel Engine (86 - 93) C to L	1857
Austin Healey 100/6 & 3000 (56 - 68) up to G *	0049
Bedford CF Petrol (69 - 87) up to E	0163
Bedford/Vauxhall Rascal & Suzuki Supercarry (86 - Oct 94) C to M	3015
BMW 316, 320 & 320i (4-cyl) (75 - Feb 83) up to Y *	0276
BMW 320, 320i, 323i & 325i (6-cyl) (Oct 77 - Sept 87) up to E	0815
BMW 3- & 5-Series Petrol (81 - 91) up to J	1948
BMW 3-Series Petrol (Apr 91 - 96) H to N	3210
BMW 3-Series Petrol (Sept 98 - 03) S to 53	4067
BMW 520i & 525e (Oct 81 - June 88) up to E	1560
BMW 525, 528 & 528i (73 - Sept 81) up to X *	0632
BMW 5-Series 6-cyl Petrol (April 96 - Aug 03) N to 03	4151
BMW 1500, 1502, 1600, 1602, 2000 & 2002 (59 - 77) up to S *	0240
Chrysler PT Cruiser Petrol (00 - 03) W to 53	4058
Citroën 2CV, Ami & Dyane (67 - 90) up to H	0196
Citroën AX Petrol & Diesel (87 - 97) D to P	3014
Citroën Berlingo & Peugeot Partner Petrol & Diesel (96 - 05) P to 55	4281
Citroën BX Petrol (83 - 94) A to L	0908
Citroën C15 Van Petrol & Diesel (89 - Oct 98) F to S	3509
Citroën C3 Petrol & Diesel (02 - 05) 51 to 05	4197
Citroën CX Petrol (75 - 88) up to F	0528
Citroën Saxo Petrol & Diesel (96 - 04) N to 54	3506
Citroën Saxo Petrol & Diesel (96 - 01) N to X	3506
Citroën Visa Petrol (79 - 88) up to F	0620
Citroën Xantia Petrol & Diesel (93 - 01) K to Y	3082
Citroën XM Petrol & Diesel (89 - 00) G to X	3451
Citroën Xsara Petrol & Diesel (97 - Sept 00) R to W	3751
Citroën Xsara Picasso Petrol & Diesel (00 - 02) W to 52	3944
Citroën ZX Diesel (91 - 98) J to S	1922
Citroën ZX Petrol (91 - 98) H to S	1881
Citroën 1.7 & 1.9 litre Diesel Engine (84 - 96) A to N	1379
Fiat 126 (73 - 87) up to E *	0305
Fiat 500 (57 - 73) up to M *	0090
Fiat Bravo & Brava Petrol (95 - 00) N to W	3572
Fiat Cinquecento (93 - 98) K to R	3501
Fiat Panda (81 - 95) up to M	0793
Fiat Punto Petrol & Diesel (94 - Oct 99) L to V	3251
Fiat Punto Petrol (Oct 99 - July 03) V to 03	4066
Fiat Regata Petrol (84 - 88) A to F	1167
Fiat Tipo Petrol (88 - 91) E to J	1625
Fiat Uno Petrol (83 - 95) up to M	0923
Fiat X1/9 (74 - 89) up to G *	0273
Ford Anglia (59 - 68) up to G *	0001
Ford Capri II (& III) 1.6 & 2.0 (74 - 87) up to E *	0283
Ford Capri II (& III) 2.8 & 3.0 V6 (74 - 87) up to E	1309
Ford Cortina Mk III 1300 & 1600 (70 - 76) up to P *	0070
Ford Escort Mk I 1100 & 1300 (68 - 74) up to N *	0171
Ford Escort Mk I Mexico, RS 1600 & RS 2000 (70 - 74) up to N *	0139
Ford Escort Mk II Mexico, RS 1800 & RS 2000 (75 - 80) up to W *	0735
Ford Escort (75 - Aug 80) up to V *	0280
Ford Escort Petrol (Sept 80 - Sept 90) up to H	0686
Ford Escort & Orion Petrol (Sept 90 - 00) H to X	1737
Ford Escort & Orion Diesel (Sept 90 - 00) H to X	4081
Ford Fiesta (76 - Aug 83) up to Y	0334
Ford Fiesta Petrol (Aug 83 - Feb 89) A to F	1030
Ford Fiesta Petrol (Feb 89 - Oct 95) F to N	1595
Ford Fiesta Petrol & Diesel (Oct 95 - Mar 02) N to 02	3397
Ford Fiesta Petrol & Diesel (Apr 02 - 05) 02 to 54	4170
Ford Focus Petrol & Diesel (98 - 01) S to Y	3759
Ford Focus Petrol & Diesel (Oct 01 - 04) 51 to 54	4167
Ford Galaxy Petrol & Diesel (95 - Aug 00) M to W	3984
Ford Granada Petrol (Sept 77 - Feb 85) up to B *	0481
Ford Granada & Scorpio Petrol (Mar 85 - 94) B to M	1245
Ford Ka (96 - 02) P to 52	3570
Ford Mondeo Petrol (93 - Sept 00) K to X	1923
Ford Mondeo Petrol & Diesel (Oct 00 - Jul 03) X to 03	3990
Ford Mondeo Diesel (93 - 96) L to N	3465
Ford Orion (83 - Sept 90) up to H	1009
Ford Sierra 4-cyl Petrol (82 - 93) up to K	0903
Ford Sierra V6 Petrol (82 - 91) up to J	0904
Ford Transit Petrol (Mk 2) (78 - Jan 86) up to C	0719
Ford Transit Petrol (Mk 3) (Feb 86 - 89) C to G	1468
Ford Transit Diesel (Feb 86 - 99) C to T	3019
Ford 1.6 & 1.8 litre Diesel Engine (84 - 96) A to N	1172
Ford 2.1, 2.3 & 2.5 litre Diesel Engine (77 - 90) up to H	1606
Freight Rover Sherpa Petrol (74 - 87) up to E	0463
Hillman Avenger (70 - 82) up to E	0037
Hillman Imp (63 - 76) up to R *	0022
Honda Civic (Feb 84 - Oct 87) A to E	1226
Honda Civic (Nov 91 - 96) J to N	3199
Honda Civic Petrol (Mar 95 - 00) M to X	4050
Hyundai Pony (85 - 94) C to M	3398
Jaguar E Type (61 - 72) up to E *	0140
Jaguar MkI & II, 240 & 340 (55 - 69) up to H *	0098
Jaguar XJ6, XJ & Sovereign; Daimler Sovereign (68 - Oct 86) up to D	0242
Jaguar XJ6 & Sovereign (Oct 86 - Sept 94) D to M	3261
Jaguar XJ12, XJS & Sovereign; Daimler Double Six (72 - 88) up to F	0478
Jeep Cherokee Petrol (93 - 96) K to N	1943
Lada 1200, 1300, 1500 & 1600 (74 - 91) up to J	0413
Lada Samara (87 - 91) D to J	1610
Land Rover 90, 110 & Defender Diesel (83 - 95) up to N	3017
Land Rover Discovery Petrol & Diesel (89 - 98) G to S	3016
Land Rover Freelander Petrol & Diesel (97 - 02) R to 52	3929
Land Rover Series IIA & III Diesel (58 - 85) up to C	0529
Land Rover Series II, IIA & III 4-cyl Petrol (58 - 85) up to C	0314
Mazda 323 (Mar 81 - Oct 89) up to G	1608
Mazda 323 (Oct 89 - 98) G to R	3455
Mazda 626 (May 83 - Sept 87) up to E	0929
Mazda B1600, B1800 & B2000 Pick-up Petrol (72 - 88) up to F	0267
Mazda RX-7 (79 - 85) up to C *	0460
Mercedes-Benz 190, 190E & 190D Petrol & Diesel (83 - 93) A to L	3450
Mercedes-Benz 200D, 240D, 240TD, 300D & 300TD 123 Series Diesel (Oct 76 - 85) up	1114
Mercedes-Benz 250 & 280 (68 - 72) up to L *	0346
Mercedes-Benz 250 & 280 123 Series Petrol (Oct 76 - 84) up to B *	0677
Mercedes-Benz 124 Series Petrol & Diesel (85 - Aug 93) C to K	3253
Mercedes-Benz C-Class Petrol & Diesel (93 - Aug 00) L to W	3511
MGA (55 - 62) *	0475
MGB (62 - 80) up to W	0111
MG Midget & Austin-Healey Sprite (58 - 80) up to W *	0265
Mini Petrol (July 01 - 05) Y to 05	4273
Mitsubishi Shogun & L200 Pick-Ups Petrol (83 - 94) up to M	1944
Morris Ital 1.3 (80 - 84) up to B	0705
Morris Minor 1000 (56 - 71) up to K	0024
Nissan Almera Petrol (95 - Feb 00) N to V	4053
Nissan Bluebird (May 84 - Mar 86) A to C	1223
Nissan Bluebird Petrol (Mar 86 - 90) C to H	1473
Nissan Cherry (Sept 82 - 86) up to D	1031
Nissan Micra (83 - Jan 93) up to K	0931
Nissan Micra (93 - 02) K to 52	3254
Nissan Micra (93 - 99) K to T	3254
Nissan Primera Petrol (90 - Aug 99) H to T	1851
Nissan Stanza (82 - 86) up to D	0824
Nissan Sunny Petrol (May 82 - Oct 86) up to D	0895
Nissan Sunny Petrol (Oct 86 - Mar 91) D to H	1378
Nissan Sunny (Apr 91 - 95) H to N	3219
Opel Ascona & Manta (B Series) (Sept 75 - 88) up to F *	0316
Opel Ascona Petrol (81 - 88)	3215
Opel Astra Petrol (Oct 91 - Feb 98)	3156
Opel Corsa Petrol (83 - Mar 93)	3160
Opel Corsa Petrol (Mar 93 - 97)	3159
Opel Kadett Petrol (Nov 79 - Oct 84) up to B	0634
Opel Kadett Petrol (Oct 84 - Oct 91)	3196
Opel Omega & Senator Petrol (86 - 94)	3157
Opel Rekord Petrol (Feb 78 - Oct 86) up to D	0543
Opel Vectra Petrol (Oct 88 - Oct 95)	3158
Peugeot 106 Petrol & Diesel (91 - 04) J to 53	1882
Peugeot 205 Petrol (83 - 97) A to P	0932
Peugeot 206 Petrol & Diesel (98 - 01) S to X	3757
Peugeot 306 Petrol & Diesel (93 - 02) K to 02	3073
Peugeot 307 Petrol & Diesel (01 - 04) Y to 54	4147
Peugeot 309 Petrol (86 - 93) C to K	1266
Peugeot 405 Petrol (88 - 97) E to P	1559
Peugeot 405 Diesel (88 - 97) E to P	3198
Peugeot 406 Petrol & Diesel (96 - Mar 99) N to T	3394
Peugeot 406 Petrol & Diesel (Mar 99 - 02) T to 52	3982
Peugeot 505 Petrol (79 - 89) up to G	0762
Peugeot 1.7/1.8 & 1.9 litre Diesel Engine (82 - 96) up to N	0950
Peugeot 2.0, 2.1, 2.3 & 2.5 litre Diesel Engines (74 - 90) up to H	1607
Porsche 911 (65 - 85) up to C	0264
Porsche 924 & 924 Turbo (76 - 85) up to C	0397
Proton (89 - 97) F to P	3255
Range Rover V8 Petrol (70 - Oct 92) up to K	0606
Reliant Robin & Kitten (73 - 83) up to A *	0436
Renault 4 (61 - 86) up to D *	0072
Renault 5 Petrol (Feb 85 - 96) B to N	1219
Renault 9 & 11 Petrol (82 - 89) up to F	0822
Renault 18 Petrol (79 - 86) up to D	0598
Renault 19 Petrol (89 - 96) F to N	1646
Renault 19 Diesel (89 - 96) F to N	1946
Renault 21 Petrol (86 - 94) C to M	1397
Renault 25 Petrol & Diesel (84 - 92) B to K	1228
Renault Clio Petrol (91 - May 98) H to R	1853
Renault Clio Diesel (91 - June 96) H to N	3031
Renault Clio Petrol & Diesel (May 98 - May 01) R to Y	3906
Renault Clio Petrol & Diesel (June 01 - 04) Y to 54	4168
Renault Espace Petrol & Diesel (85 - 96) C to N	3197
Renault Laguna Petrol & Diesel (94 - 00) L to W	3252
Renault Mégane & Scénic Petrol & Diesel (96 - 98) N to R	3395
Renault Mégane & Scénic Petrol & Diesel (Apr 99 - 02) T to 52	3916
Renault Megane Petrol & Diesel (Oct 02 - 05) 52 to 55	4284
Renault Scenic Petrol & Diesel (Sept 03 - 06) 53 to 06	4297
Rover 213 & 216 (84 - 89) A to G	1116
Rover 214 & 414 (89 - 96) G to N	1689
Rover 216 & 416 Petrol (89 - 96) G to N	1830
Rover 211, 214, 216, 218 & 220 Petrol & Diesel (Dec 95 - 99) N to V	3399
Rover 25 & MG ZR Petrol & Diesel (Oct 99 - 04) V to 54	4145
Rover 414, 416 & 420 Petrol & Diesel (May 95 - 98) M to R	3453
Rover 618, 620 & 623 Petrol (93 - 97) K to P	3257
Rover 820, 825 & 827 Petrol (86 - 95) D to N	1380
Rover 3500 (76 - 87) up to E	0365
Rover Metro, 111 & 114 Petrol (May 90 - 98) G to S	1711
Saab 95 & 96 (66 - 76) up to R *	0198
Saab 90, 99 & 900 (79 - Oct 93) up to L	0765
Saab 900 (Oct 93 - 98) L to R	3512
Saab 9000 (4-cyl) (85 - 98) C to S	1686
Saab 9-5 4-cyl Petrol (97 - 04) R to 54	4156
Seat Ibiza & Cordoba Petrol & Diesel (Oct 93 - Oct 99) L to V	3571
Seat Ibiza & Malaga Petrol (85 - 92) B to K	1609
Skoda Estelle (77 - 89) up to G	0604
Skoda Favorit (89 - 96) F to N	1801
Skoda Felicia Petrol & Diesel (95 - 01) M to X	3505
Subaru 1600 & 1800 (Nov 79 - 90) up to H *	0995
Sunbeam Alpine, Rapier & H120 (67 - 74) up to N *	0051
Suzuki SJ Series, Samurai & Vitara (4-cyl) Petrol (82 - 97) up to P	1942
Talbot Alpine, Solara, Minx & Rapier (75 - 86) up to D	0337
Talbot Horizon Petrol (78 - 86) up to D	0473
Talbot Samba (82 - 86) up to D	0823
Toyota Carina E Petrol (May 92 - 97) J to P	3256
Toyota Corolla (80 - 85) up to C	0683
Toyota Corolla (Sept 83 - Sept 87) A to E	1024
Toyota Corolla (Sept 87 - Aug 92) E to K	1683
Toyota Corolla Petrol (Aug 92 - 97) K to P	3259
Toyota Hi-Ace & Hi-Lux Petrol (69 - Oct 83) up to A	0304
Toyota Yaris Petrol (99 - 05) T to 05	4265
Triumph GT6 & Vitesse (62 - 74) up to N *	0112
Triumph Herald (59 - 71) up to K *	0010
Triumph Spitfire (62 - 81) up to N *	0113
Triumph Stag (70 - 78) up to T *	0441
Triumph TR2, TR3, TR3A, TR4 & TR4A (52 - 67) up to F *	0028
Triumph TR5 & 6 (67 - 75) up to P *	0031
Triumph TR7 (75 - 82) up to Y *	0322
Vauxhall Astra Petrol (80 - Oct 84) up to B	0635
Vauxhall Astra & Belmont Petrol (Oct 84 - Oct 91) B to J	1136
Vauxhall Astra Petrol (Oct 91 - Feb 98) J to R	1832
Vauxhall/Opel Astra & Zafira Petrol (Feb 98 - Apr 04) R to 04	3758
Vauxhall/Opel Astra & Zafira Diesel (Feb 98 - Apr 04) R to 04	3797
Vauxhall/Opel Calibra (90 - 98) G to S	3502
Vauxhall Carlton Petrol (Oct 78 - Oct 86) up to D	0480
Vauxhall Carlton & Senator Petrol (Nov 86 - 94) D to L	1469
Vauxhall Cavalier Petrol (81 - Oct 88) up to F	0812
Vauxhall Cavalier Petrol (Oct 88 - 95) F to N	1570
Vauxhall Chevette (75 - 84) up to B	0285
Vauxhall/Opel Corsa Petrol (Mar 93 - Oct 00) K to X	4087
Vauxhall Corsa Petrol (Mar 93 - 97) K to R	1985
Vauxhall/Opel Corsa Petrol (Apr 97 - Oct 00) P to X	3921
Vauxhall/Opel Corsa Petrol & Diesel (Oct 00 - Sept 03) X to 53	4079
Vauxhall/Opel Frontera Petrol & Diesel (91 - Sept 98) J to S	3454
Vauxhall Nova Petrol (83 - 93) up to K	0909
Vauxhall/Opel Omega Petrol (94 - 99) L to T	3510
Vauxhall/Opel Vectra Petrol & Diesel (95 - Feb 99) N to S	3396
Vauxhall/Opel Vectra Petrol & Diesel (Mar 99 - May 02) T to 02	3930
Vauxhall/Opel 1.5, 1.6 & 1.7 litre Diesel Engine (82 - 96) up to N	1222
Volkswagen 411 & 412 (68 - 75) up to P *	0091
Volkswagen Beetle 1200 (54 - 77) up to S	0036
Volkswagen Beetle 1300 & 1500 (65 - 75) up to P	0039
Volkswagen Beetle 1302 & 1302S (70 - 72) up to L *	0110
Volkswagen Beetle 1303, 1303S & GT (72 - 75) up to P	0159
Volkswagen Beetle Petrol & Diesel (Apr 99 - 01) T to 51	3798
Volkswagen Golf & Bora Petrol & Diesel (April 98 - 00) R to X	3727
Volkswagen Golf & Jetta Mk 1 Petrol 1.1 & 1.3 (74 - 84) up to A	0716
Volkswagen Golf, Jetta & Scirocco Mk 1 Petrol 1.5, 1.6 & 1.8 (74 - 84) up to A	0726
Volkswagen Golf & Jetta Mk 1 Diesel (78 - 84) up to A	0451
Volkswagen Golf & Jetta Mk 2 Petrol (Mar 84 - Feb 92) A to J	1081
Volkswagen Golf & Vento Petrol & Diesel (Feb 92 - Mar 98) J to R	3097
Volkswagen Golf & Bora 4-cyl Petrol & Diesel (01 - 03) X to 53	4169
Volkswagen LT Petrol Vans & Light Trucks (76 - 87) up to E	0637
Volkswagen Passat & Santana Petrol (Sept 81 - May 88) up to E	0814
Volkswagen Passat 4-cyl Petrol & Diesel (May 88 - 96) E to P	3498
Volkswagen Passat 4-cyl Petrol & Diesel (Dec 96 - Nov 00) P to X	3917
VW Passat Petrol & Diesel (Dec 00 - May 05) X to 05	4279
Volkswagen Polo & Derby (76 - Jan 82) up to X	0335
Volkswagen Polo (82 - Oct 90) up to H	0813
Volkswagen Polo Petrol (Nov 90 - Aug 94) H to L	3245
Volkswagen Polo Hatchback Petrol & Diesel (94 - 99) M to S	3500
Volkswagen Polo Hatchback Petrol (00 - Jan 02) V to 51	4150
Volkswagen Scirocco (82 - 90) up to H *	1224
Volkswagen Transporter 1600 (68 - 79) up to V	0082
Volkswagen Transporter 1700, 1800 & 2000 (72 - 79) up to V *	0226
Volkswagen Transporter (air-cooled) Petrol (79 - 82) up to Y *	0638
Volkswagen Transporter (water-cooled) Petrol (82 - 90) up to H	3452
Volkswagen Type 3 (63 - 73) up to M *	0084
Volvo 120 & 130 Series (& P1800) (61 - 73) up to M *	0203
Volvo 142, 144 & 145 (66 - 74) up to N *	0129
Volvo 240 Series Petrol (74 - 93) up to K	0270
Volvo 262, 264 & 260/265 (75 - 85) up to C *	0400
Volvo 340, 343, 345 & 360 (76 - 91) up to J	0715
Volvo 440, 460 & 480 Petrol (87 - 97) D to P	1691
Volvo 740 & 760 Petrol (82 - 91) up to J	1258
Volvo 850 Petrol (92 - 96) J to P	3260
Volvo 940 Petrol (90 - 96) H to N	3249
Volvo S40 & V40 Petrol (96 - Mar 04) N to 04	3569
Volvo S70, V70 & C70 Petrol (96 - 99) P to V	3573
Volvo V70 / S80 Petrol & Diesel (98 - 05) S to 55	4263

* = Classic Reprints